DUCTED FANS
FOR
MODEL JETS

Dedication

To my wife, Margaret, who has not only put up with my obsession to a far greater extent than I ever deserved, but has also helped unselfishly with the preparation of this book and the operation of our small company.

Acknowledgements

Although I have generally acknowledged specific contributions at the appropriate place in the text, I would like to thank particularly the following individuals and organisations for the provision of information, drawings and photographs:

Philip Avonds, Mike Billinton, Chart Micromold, Alec Cornish-Trestrail, Rolf Gleichauf, Bruce Godberson, Chris Golds, Bob Kress, Marcus Norman (deceased), Robart Manufacturing, Phil Smith, Ron Sweeney, Peter and Paul Thorpe, Veron (Solarbo Ltd), Bob Violett, Larry Wolfe.

DUCTED FANS
FOR
MODEL JETS

David James

ARGUS BOOKS

Argus Books
Argus House
Boundary Way
Hemel Hempstead
Hertfordshire HP2 7ST
England

First published by Argus Books 1989
Reprinted 1993
© David James 1989

ISBN 0 85242 977 0

The cover shows a large ducted fan model of an F-14 Tomcat built by a group of Belgian modellers. It features a variable wing sweep mechanism and weighs about 30 pounds. The fullsize Tomcat was the star performer in the movie 'Top Gun'.

Phototypesetting by The Works, Exeter, Devon. EX4 3LS, England.

Printed and bound in Great Britain by Biddles Ltd., Guildford and King's Lynn

CONTENTS

Foreword

1 Introduction to Ducted Fans   8

2 Fan Theory and Design   24

3 The Ducted Fan Unit   43

4 The Engine   61

5 The Airframe   79

6 Auxiliary Systems   117

7 Operation   128

8 Kits and Plans   147

9 The Future   158

Appendix 1   Manufacturers and Suppliers Addresses   163

Appendix 2   Ducted Fan References   165

Index   173

FOREWORD

Having formed a small company in 1982, dedicated to that very specialised corner of the aeromodelling market occupied by ducted fans, I have been made aware of the tremendous growth of interest in this exciting facet of our hobby. Each week brings its quota of telephone calls and letters, of which perhaps three-quarters are concerned with information rather than business, although business often follows once the thirst for knowledge has been satisfied.

It isn't difficult to see why many of the enquiries seem naive or downright confused — until recently there have been virtually no specialised publications covering this new technology. I have prepared information packages, published articles and produced videos, but what was clearly needed was a standard reference work that could serve both as a useful introduction to ducted fan technology and be consulted from time to time as the reader's involvement and experience increases.

Space and time do not allow a comprehensive treatment of all the foundation blocks of conventional aeromodelling; there is in any case no real shortage of such material on the bookshelves. Instead, I have chosen to concentrate on those features that are unique to ducted fans assuming that the reader has built and flown at least one radio-controlled model aircraft and, preferably, has experience of a reasonably fast 'foam and fibreglass' model.

As well as the rather basic questions asked by modellers contemplating ducted fans for the first time, I also receive many requests from experienced 'jet-jockies' requiring reference material covering more advanced aspects of the art. They may wish to know, for instance, if anyone has built a swing-wing Tomcat and how did he overcome the trim change as the wing moves back and forth, or whether plans are available for a DH 110, or how to design a thrust reverser.

The answers to such questions are almost always available in articles published in various magazines around the world. The difficulty is knowing where to find them. Therefore, I have included a list of more than 300 such articles at the back of this book. The reader should be able to obtain back copies from the magazine publisher or from certain specialist aviation bookshops. Failing that, a visit to a major reference library such as the National Reference Library in Chancery Lane, London, could help. In a last act of desperation, try a letter to me. Although every attempt has been made to keep the list accurate, the reader is advised to check with the supplier that the magazine article he orders does, indeed, contain the reference material he needs.

Finally, a list of ducted fan manufacturers and suppliers is provided in Appendix 1. The addresses should be accurate at the time of going to press.

David James
1989

1 INTRODUCTION TO DUCTED FANS

1.1 General background

I would not be the first person to observe that aeromodellers tend to build models of full-size aircraft that occupied the skies of their youth. The advance of full-size aviation has not been slow nor has it gone hand-in-hand with simplicity. Therefore, it is not surprising that model aviation has been hard pressed to keep pace with its bigger brother. Nowhere has this technology gap been more acute than in the field of jet-powered aircraft. There are many modellers who reached maturity in the years following the last World War who must have felt frustration while contemplating the graceful flowing lines of the early swept-wing jets, knowing that there was no way that they could ever simulate such appearance and performance in a model. It was one thing to put a propeller on a diesel and go fly a Spitfire, but where could they find a jet engine?

There have been many attempts over the past forty years to build miniature gas turbines capable of model jet aircraft propulsion. All have been doomed to failure or obscurity until comparatively recently when improvements in machining, materials and fabrication technology have allowed small, high precision, multibladed turbine and compressor wheels to be produced. These components are at the heart of the jet engine and, when coupled together by a shaft, form the only moving parts in a much simpler machine than the reciprocating internal combustion engine, typified by the model glow or diesel engines with which we are so familiar.

Conceptual simplicity is one thing, engineering reality is another, as Sir Frank Whittle discovered during his pioneering work on the first successful jet engines. As well as fabricational problems, the other main technical barriers are the high temperatures and high rotational

TABLE 1.1 COMPARISON OF MINIATURE GAS TURBINES

NAME	G. JACKMAN	KUESTER	TURBOMIN 100	STEVE ROSE	CONTINENTAL RPV	KAVAN	SEEGERS	BOOZ
COUNTRY	UK	USA	SWEDEN	UK	USA	W.GER	USA	USA
WEIGHT (pounds)	4	4.5	6.6	13	14	17	5.6	—
THRUST (pounds)	9 at 85,000 rpm 18 max. (take-off)	—	22	28	47	55	11 at 69,000 rpm 14 at 80,000 rpm	12 at 95,000 rpm
DIAMETER (inches)	4.75	5.24	6	6.25	6.5	6	5.5	6
LENGTH (inches)	13.5	—	12	13	12	17	11.5	—
RPM (Max.)	110,000	100,000	105,000	100,000	97,000	96,000	80,000	95,000
PRESSURE RATIO	2:1	2.2:1	2.3:1	3:1	—	—	—	—
EXHAUST TEMP (°C)	650	788	700	760	—	—	—	550
AIRFLOW (pounds/sec)	—	0.7	0.57	—	—	1.11	—	—
FUEL	PROPANE	KEROSENE/ GASOLINE or PROPANE	KEROSENE	—	KEROSENE	GASOLINE	GASOLINE	PROPANE
FLOWN?	YES	NO	NO	—	YES	YES	YES	—

Fig. 1.1. In 1982, Gerry Jackman's miniature gas turbine was the first successfully to power a radio-controlled model aircraft.

speeds involved. It took half a century for model aviation to match Whittle's achievement when Gerry Jackman flew his gas turbine powered BARJAY before a large crowd at the 1982 Ducted Fan Fly-in at Abingdon (Fig. 1.1). No-one can ever rob Gerry of this crowning glory born of so many years of toil, disappointment and near despair with very meagre resources at his disposal. Today there are still only a handful of model gas turbine designs around the world, and even fewer have flown. Table 1.1, gives a partial list of such engines. Automobile turbocharger development has helped a lot as the technology is so similar to the gas turbine and, very recently, small turbines built to propel missiles have been used to fly models. Such engines are still very expensive, of course, but who knows what might develop if one of the model engine manufacturers from Japan or Taiwan, for example, decide to enter the mass production market?

For the moment, however, we must content ourselves with humbler methods of propulsion. I will not dwell on the various forms of pulse jet, ram jet, duct jet and pressure jets that have found limited application in models, as they all suffer from one or more of the following problems — restricted availability, legality, noise and safety — although there remains a number of dedicated enthusiasts for this type of engine, scattered around the world.

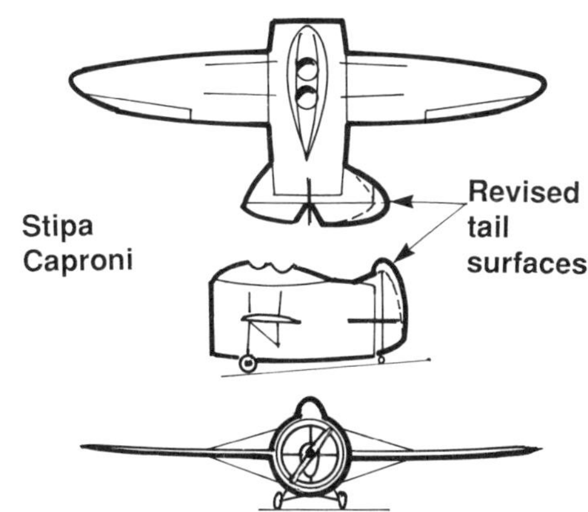

Fig. 1.2. Italian STIPA-CAPRONI I ducted airscrew aircraft showing original and revised tail surfaces.

1.2 History

An air of mystery surrounds the earliest successful use of ducted fans, although there is little doubt that the first model flights took place in the United Kingdom. As far back as 1927, Ing. Stipa of Italy began investigating the possibility of a venturi-tube fuselage as a means of improving propeller thrust. The resulting aircraft (Fig. 1.2) had a length of 20 feet and a diameter of 8 feet. Little is known about the performance of this extraordinary aircraft but it was almost certainly disappointing, as there appears to have been no further development of the type.

About a year before writing this book I received a visit from Marcus Norman. He had brought with him a trophy that he had dedicated to the memory of his father, the late P. E. Norman. Marcus wanted the trophy to be awarded at the Annual Ducted Fan Fly-in at Abingdon to the modeller judged by his peers to have built and flown the most innovative and successful model demonstrated at the event. Marcus also brought with him some articles chronicling his father's early achievements with ducted fans. He promised to let me have more information, but his untimely, tragic death a few months later in an air accident, robbed aviation of one of its most creative and colourful characters.

By pure coincidence, a few weeks after Marcus's visit I received a letter and information from Phil Smith who was, for 34 years, designer for Veron, the British kit manufacturer. His experiments began while he worked for *Aeromodeller* magazine shortly after the war. His first ducted fan kit was produced in 1948 — a Lavochkin LA 17. The fans

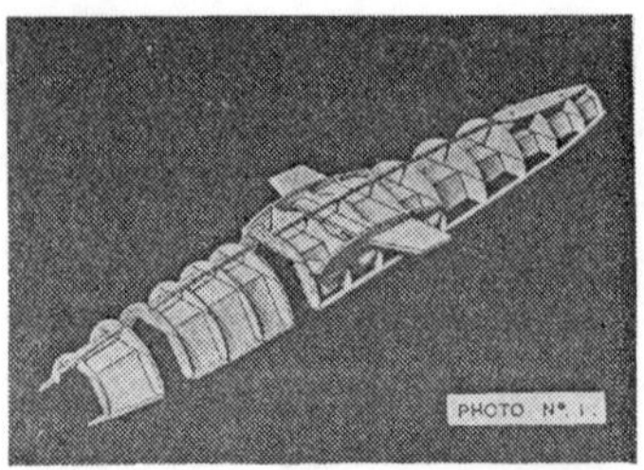

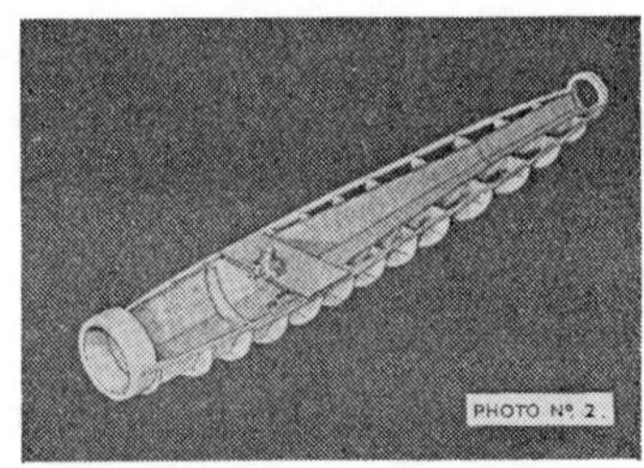

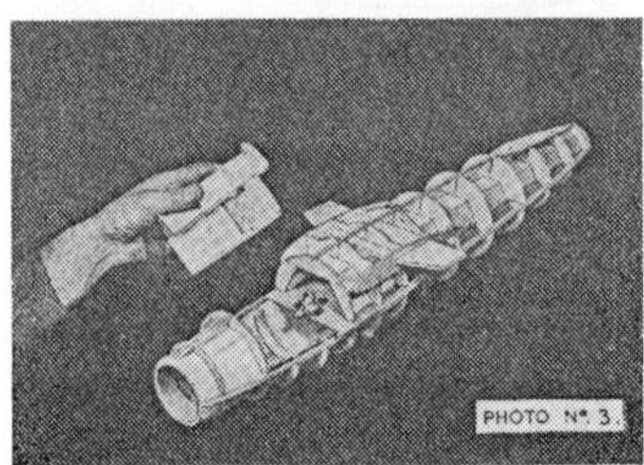

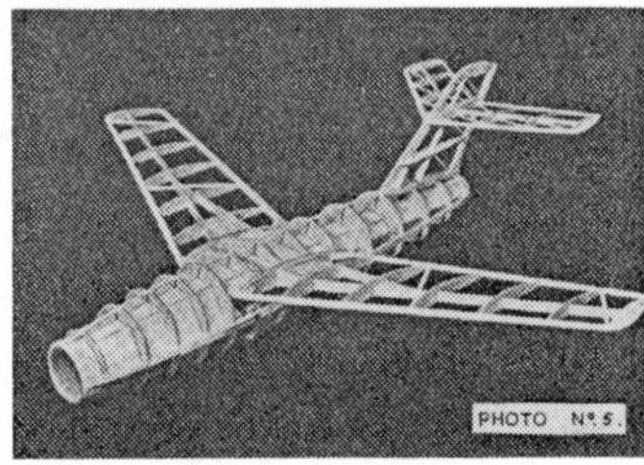

Fig. 1.3. Vintage modellers will appreciate details extracted from Veron's instructions for the Lavochkin LA-17. The first ducted fan kit in the world, designed by Phil Smith in 1948.

were made from aluminium (against his own personal judgement) instead of annealed Duralumin, and proved to be subject to fatigue failures. He then produced handmade impellers utilizing fibre blades and plywood hubs. Production ran to thousands, many of them being used by electrical equipment manufacturers, such as Marconi, for humidity control purposes.

Phil Smith's early work with Veron was more or less concurrent with an American modeller, Thomas H. Purcell Jnr., who produced a Skyray kit which was later manufactured by Berkeley Models in the USA. Bill Effinger and Henry Struck also developed ducted fan models for the same company. Until 1972, however, the Veron fan was the only commercial unit available.

The Veron Lavochkin (Fig. 1.3) was unusual in having a hexagonal duct; in most other respects, however, it established broad principles of design that are still with us 40 years later. The instructions accompanying the kit refer to " . . . . . a new and intriguing method of propulsion, the IMP SYSTEM, being a diesel or glowplug powered ducted impeller." Had it not been for the subsequent involvement of Americans in the new technology, this book might be titled 'Ducted Imps'!

To return to the Lavochkin, it was intended that the fan blades could be twisted so as to suit all capacities of motor from 0.5 to 0.9 cc. A half-ounce fuel tank was suggested and starting was effected by "..24 inches of stout string." The typical flight was described as "....a long gradual climb in wide circles, resembling true jet flight", although contemporary reports suggest that an extended powered glide was more frequently achieved. Although the Lavochkin was kitted in 1948, there are reports of electric ducted fan experiments by G.W.W. Harris and Squadron Leader Peter Short dating back to 1945 (Fig 1.4), although it is not clear whether successful flights were achieved.

For most would-be jet modellers of that period, the ubiquitous JETEX motor represented the only practical means of simulating jet flight and, once again, Veron pioneered the way with very successful models of the F-86 Sabre, Thunderjet, Sea-hawk, and Supermarine Attacker. These models provided very good value for money and it is particularly satisfying to note that the JETEX motor and small free-flight kits are once again available to attract a new generation of aeromodellers into our fascinating hobby.

While these developments were proceeding in the commercial world, P. E. Norman's ideas were bearing fruit in the private sector. In the *Aeromodeller Annual* for 1955, he describes his first impeller of 4⅛ inch diameter made from aluminium sheet and prone to failure "through crystallisation" in less than two minutes. His first model was a 36-inch span MiG-15 of planked balsa construction covered with parachute silk. The complete fin and tailplane assembly was detachable (or knock-offable in the event of a hard landing). The fan unit was an integral part of the fuselage, permanently fixed in place, and the fuel tank was made from a portion of transparent toothbrush case. P. E. does not describe the flight characteristics of his first MiG but does mention that it was "...unfortunately destroyed when a car ran over it". His second MiG was similar though lighter, initially; oil seepage changed that, however, as the weight gradually increased from 24 to 29 ounces.

P. E. went on to make a Boulton Paul P 120 delta, followed by a Hawker P 1081. Engine size increased to 2.5 cc, and new 5½ inch fibre-bladed impellers were shown to be far better than the earlier aluminium types. The problem of thrust-to-weight ratio was becoming apparent and the next model was a Mystère II having several cheat intakes to provide extra thrust at the expense of scale appearance and a tendency to stall. The latter problem was corrected by providing a cheat *outlet* which changed the thrustline to provide a little downthrust.

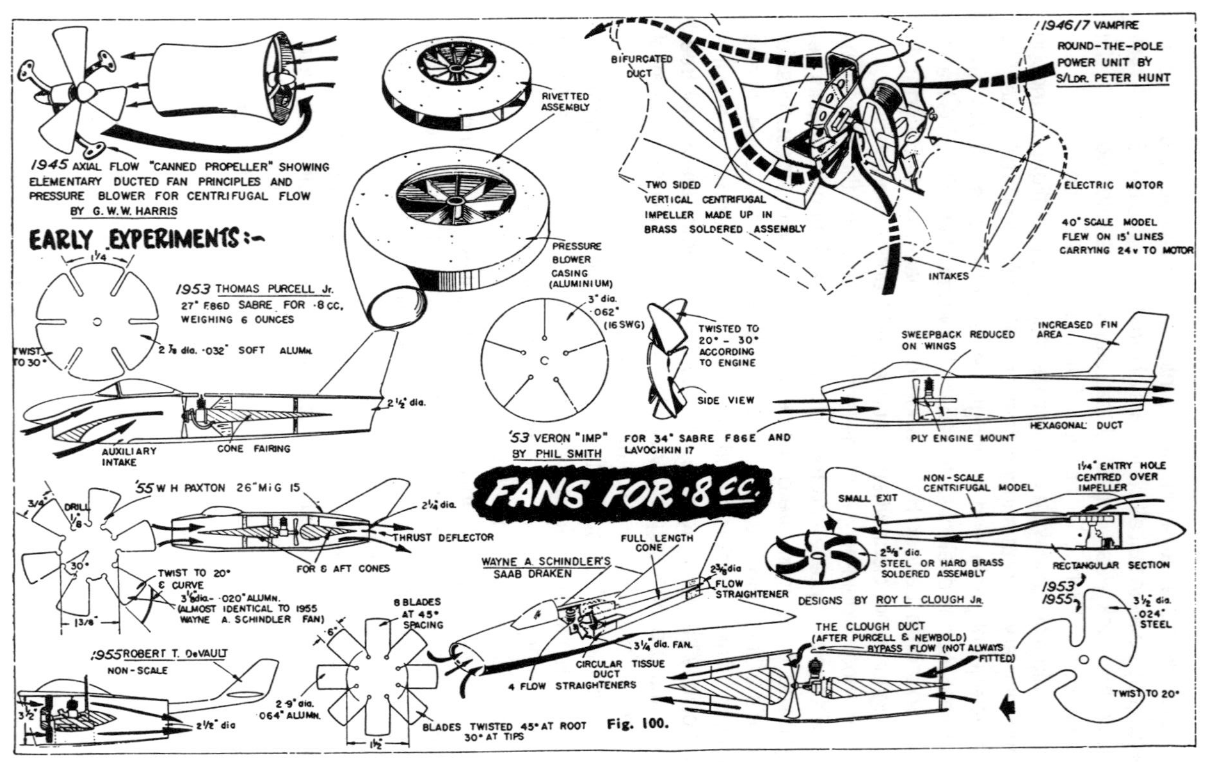

Fig. 1.4. Showing some of the early aluminium impeller designs and methods of installation in ducted fan models.

There followed a Hunter, later transmogrified into a Cougar (P. E. was noted for his ingenuity and artistic flair). This used a centrifugal impeller but the flight characteristics did not encourage further development of this type of fan. His next model was a Boulton Paul P IIIA Delta which utilised a novel rolled-tube construction covered with one of his wife's nylon stockings (a 'throw-out' he hastened to add). The model was very successful, being both fast and stable.

A Cougar, a Yak 25 and two more MiG-15s (Fig. 1.5) followed, the last one being fabricated from fibre-glass which turned out to be approximately the same weight as the wooden version, but considerably stronger and not subject to oil seepage. P. E. then produced a list of problems that needed to be overcome. Most of them are still with us (vibration, engine wear, power-to-weight ratio etc.) but curiously he also mentioned that "...ducted fan models have a marked torque and gyroscopic reaction". This contrasts with the view expressed in so many recent articles that ducted fans are characterised by their lack of torque effects thereby allowing perfectly axial rolls etc. P. E. was right, of course, in that the impeller could not turn without torque being applied to it, and this was very obvious in those far-off free-flight days when the art of trimming was so important.

P. E. Norman's next excursion into print seems to be in 1962 in *American Modeller* magazine. By then, he had established certain bench marks for fan design: roughly 5 inch diameter, 6 to 8 fibre blades, 40° to 45° pitch at the root, powered by a high-revving glow engine rather than one of his earlier diesel engines. Engine size had risen to 5.5cc and all-up weight to almost 4 pounds, but the really exciting news was that he had built and flown a number of radio-controlled ducted fan aircraft. They were capable of taking off under their own power (using a dolly), could achieve 50 mph in flight, and were easy to fly. He won a spot landing competition with his first R/C ducted fan in 1959.

By the time he died at the early age of 52, on July 5th 1964, P. E. Norman had built over 30 ducted fan models. As his son Marcus remarked in a moving obituary "Aeromodelling to Dad was not just a hobby but an obsession...", an obsession that Marcus inherited and carried with him throughout his tragically short, creative life.

By 1974, Marcus had pushed back the frontiers of ducted fan technology with several designs which were natural developments of his father's concepts. This was not before he had tried several revolutionary ideas all of which were doomed to oblivion. However, P. E. would no doubt have smiled at his son's perversity and been even more delighted when the painful lessons had been learned.

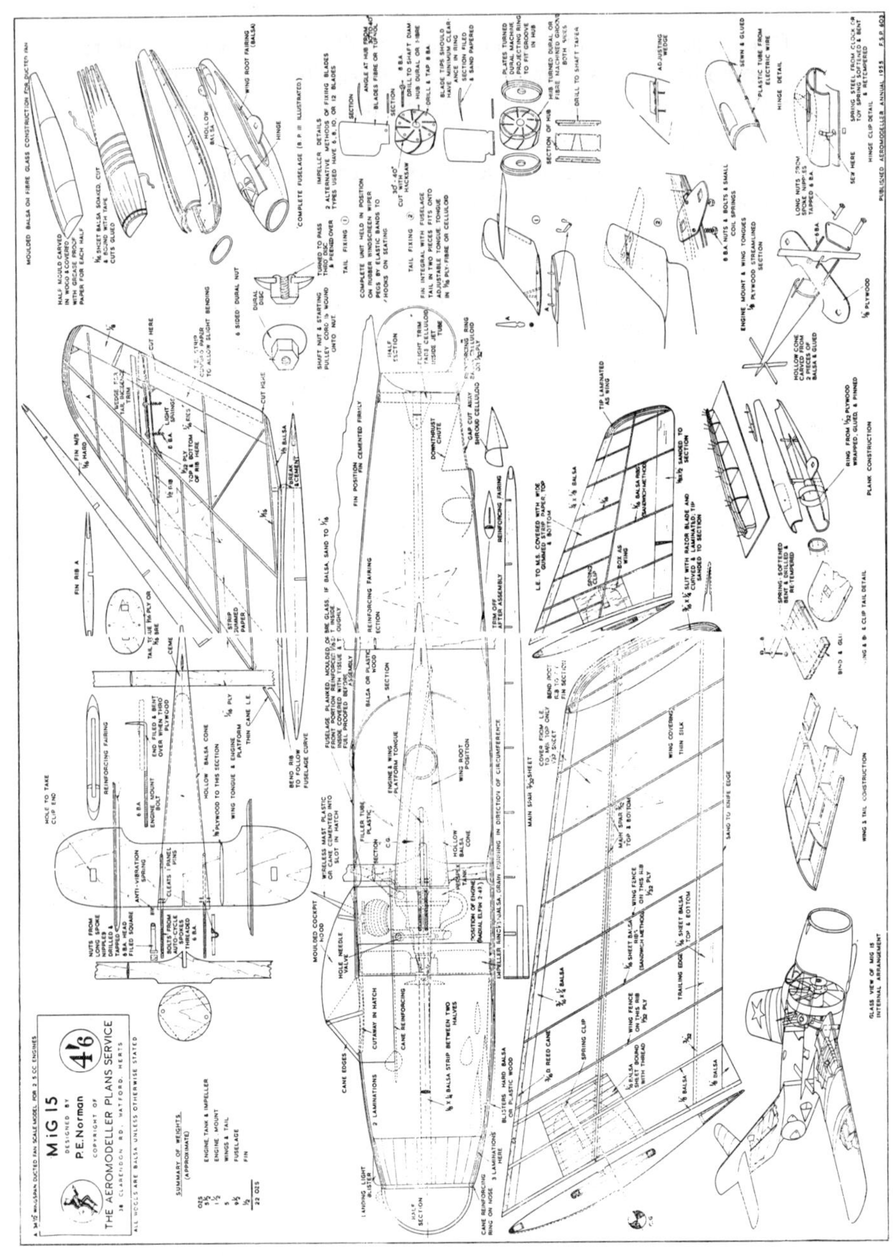

Fig. 1.5. Reproduction of Aeromodeller Plan for P.E. Norman's MiG-15. (Aeromodeller Annual 1955).

Marcus's main contribution derived from his systematic approach to fan design. This was entirely experimental and depended on simple spring balance thrust measurements coupled with careful flight observations. He quickly realised that, if high efficiency was to be achieved, the impeller rpm had to match the rpm at which the engine reached its peak horsepower. This meant developing a somewhat smaller fan and searching for engines with more and more horsepower. In turn, this meant that improved methods and materials of impeller construction were needed. Fortunately, the plastics industry provided him with just what he wanted in Permaglass and Polycarbonate materials for the blades, and the pylon racing fraternity encouraged the production of extremely fast 'forties' like the K&B 40 engine.

Marcus also realised the importance of duct inlet and outlet areas and provided simple design guidelines for the practitioner. Finally, he understood the importance of stator blades (or flow straighteners) for recovering some of the swirl energy in the jet efflux, thus improving fan efficiency considerably.

On the other side of the Atlantic, things were developing very rapidly culminating in the release of the SCOZZI ducted fan to the US market in 1974. When coupled to Bob Violett's famous 'Sundowner' airframe it demonstrated top speeds exceeding 80 mph and a full range of aerobatics, at the Lakehurst Scale Championships that year. The availability of a true commercial ducted fan unit complete with engine mount, shroud and stator blades gave a tremendous boost to the hobby. Now the enthusiast could visit his Hobby shop, buy his fan unit off the shelf and start building jets. It says a great deal for James Scozzafarva's original design that it is still selling well as the rugged and reliable TURBAX I marketed now by Jet Hangar Hobbies (Fig 1.6)

Scozzafarva's approach to ducted fan design was different to the experimental techniques of Marcus Norman, in that he took well-established engineering principles based on Sir Issac Newton's laws of motion and used them to calculate optimum blade sizes, numbers, angles and fan outlet diameter. Using the same K&B 40 engine and fan diameter as Marcus, Scozzafarva could achieve much greater thrusts (typically up to 8 pounds of static thrust). Engine speeds reached 21,000 rpm and tuned pipes were 'de rigeur'.

Bob Kress, chief project engineer of Grumman's F-14 Tomcat, was not slow to realise the value of a sound engineering approach, and he subsequently produced a range of fans extending from .049 up to .45 engine size. This was the famous RK series of fans, some of which

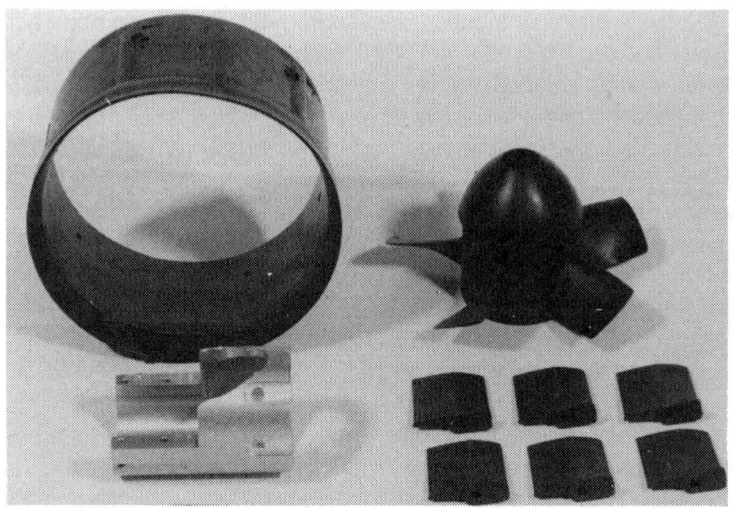

Fig. 1.6. The first successful commercial fan in the USA was the Scozzi fan on which the TURBAX I fan unit was based.

Fig. 1.7. Bob Kress designed this diminutive RK049 ducted fan unit.

are still in production today (Fig. 1.7). Bob's chief contribution will be remembered as his careful experimental evaluation of design features, such as intake size and geometry. His erudite exposition of fan theory has yet to be surpassed — a matter that we will return to later.

Continental Europe was now beginning to sit up and take notice. Within a relatively short period, the BOSS fan (Fig. 1.8) was being manufactured in Sweden followed by the BAUER fans in Germany. The former was a relatively large 12-bladed fan designed to absorb

Fig. 1.8. The first commercial fan unit produced in Continental Europe, the Swedish BOSS fan.

Fig. 1.9. The BAUER fan manufactured in West Germany was designed to utilize the power of non-racing engines operating at relatively low rpm

the power of a racing .60 size engine, whereas the BAUER fans (Fig. 1.9) were intended for use with standard sports engines operating at much lower rpm. In America, Byron Originals decided that the pusher configuration was the way to go and produced the highly successful

Fig. 1.10. The American **BYROJET** jet fan is currently the largest diameter unit being manufactured.

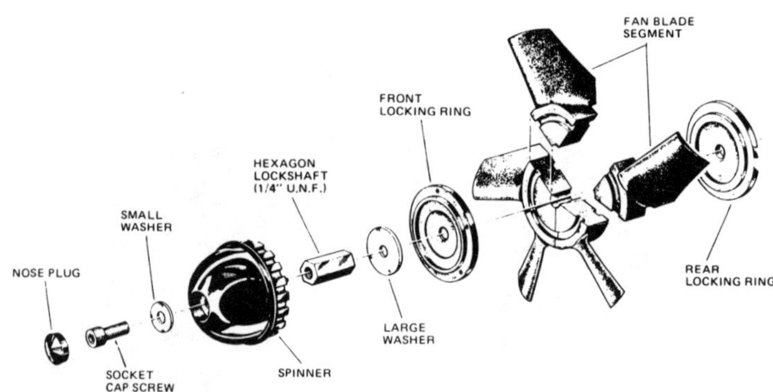

Fig. 1.11. The **MICROMOLD** fan unit was based on the home-made designs of Marcus Norman.

BYROJET (Fig. 1.10). At 6 inches impeller diameter, this is one of the largest fans, and can absorb the power of the most potent .90 size engines. In the UK, MICROMOLD produced their excellent and inexpensive fan unit based on the Norman designs (Fig. 1.11).

This burgeoning commercial activity led to the release of many practical scale kits. Bob Violett's A4 Skyhawk appeared in 1976, the first new kit since the Veron and Berkeley series in the early 1950s. Larry Wolfe of Jet Hangar Hobbies produced his first kit, the Grumman Cougar, and Byron Originals released their MiG-15.

In the early 80s, Turbofan and Fanjets in the UK produced their first

Fig. 1.12. One of the largest and most impressive models to grace the ducted fan scene. Chris Golds' 32 pound, 14 feet long Concorde.

kits. The Thorpe Brothers were busily marketing designs for a variety of scale jets and ultimately manufactured their own THORJET ducted fan unit utilizing the Micromold impeller.

There were still relatively few specialised ducted fan engines, however. Prior to 1980, the well known K&B 7.5 engine was the only one available but, with the obvious growth in the fan market, OS, Rossi, OPS and more recently Picco started to produce specialised ducted fan engines.

By 1980 it was clear that ducted fans had come of age. No longer were they the province of a few dedicated pioneers. Anyone with reasonable practical capability could build, fly and even design ducted fan aircraft successfully. With this release of inventive talent, more and more sophisticated aircraft began to appear in the magazines even though they were not often to be seen on the flying fields. A move towards larger aircraft could be detected, in keeping with a more general trend to bigger and heavier prop-driven aircraft. Multi-engine types became quite common as well as models featuring all the gimmicks and gewgaws of smoke systems, drogue 'chutes, dive brakes, thrust reversers etc. Typical of these 'state of the art' scale models are Chris Golds' magnificent 32 pound, four-engined BAC Concorde complete with droop nose (Fig. 1.12) and Canadian, Dr Jack Tse's awe inspiring swing-wing F-14 Tomcat (Fig. 1.13) so impressively displayed at the 1987 Belleville Jet Rally.

Fig. 1.13. State of the art technology exemplified. Canadian Dr. Jack Tse poses with his swing wing F-14 Tomcat. Hopefully to be kitted soon.

Fig. 1.14. Bob Violett's latest creation; the Viper. Reputed to be capable of 180 mph in level flight.

Fig. 1.15. This is what gives the Viper all that urge. The computer designed VIOJETT operates at 85% efficiency and represents the most sophisticated fan unit available today.

The chief discernible trend at present is towards very high performance sports type jets with flight envelopes typified by Bob Violett's latest creation, the Viper (Fig. 1.14). This aircraft is capable of speeds ranging from 25 to 175 mph. It features space-age carbon fibre and relies upon the most sophisticated fan and engine package the modelling world has yet seen. The VIOJETT (Fig. 1.15) could be regarded as a third generation fan unit. Computer designed by a professional power plant engineer, it converts 4½ bhp into thrust with amazing efficiency using a remarkably small 4.6 inch diameter impeller. The small size is also good news for scale enthusiasts, as it allows scale intakes and outlets without the need for cheater holes provided that care is taken with the design of the inlet duct.

There now seems to be no technological limit to the type of aircraft that can be modelled except, perhaps, the true VTO aircraft such as the Harrier, but more of that later.

2 FAN THEORY AND DESIGN

2.1 Description of a typical fan unit

A ducted fan is simply a device for accelerating air as it passes through a duct or shroud (Fig. 2.1). The duct serves primarily to limit radial flow outwards from the hub to the blade tip, thereby increasing the axial flow of air through the duct. The air is accelerated by a multibladed impeller and the swirl, or rotational component of the flow, is usually converted back to an axial flow by a further row of blades which are stationary and hence referred to as the stator. These three components — duct, impeller and stator (Fig 2.2) — are really all there is to a typical ducted fan, so this chapter will be devoted to the design and fabrication of these components and the way they interact to convert the power of the drive unit (usually a small glow motor) into thrust that can be used to propel an aircraft.

2.2 Theory

The fan unit described above can be likened to a simple single-stage, axial flow compressor. It differs from other, more familiar, compressors in that the pressure rise across it is quite small, typically a ratio of less than 1.1 from inlet to outlet, which compares to ratios of 3 to 30 for a turbocharger or gas turbine, for example. These higher pressure ratios are really only required if the unit is being used to compress a fuel and air charge prior to combustion, which is not the prime function of a model ducted fan unit. To digress for a moment, however; when the glow motor is placed behind the fan there is a small increase in power and efficiency due to the supercharging effect of the increased pressure around the carburettor inlet. To digress yet further, Sir Frank Whittle's earliest ideas for jet propulsion utilized a centrifugal fan driven by a reciprocating engine rather than a turbine. He envisaged using the rear duct as a flame tube into which gasoline could be injected and ignited. The idea was abandoned at an early

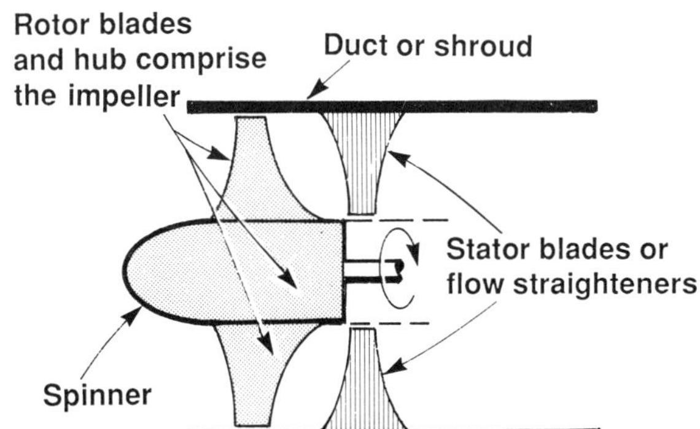

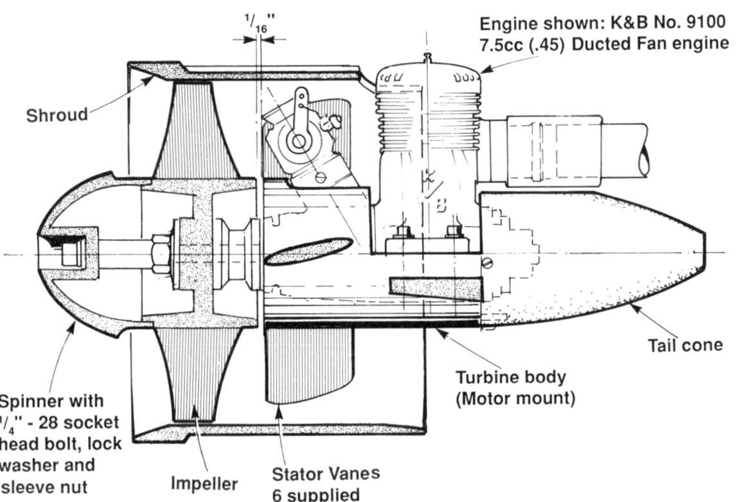

Fig. 2.2. Commercial ducted fan unit (TURBAX I) with all components identified.

stage due to the limited pressure rise that could be obtained across the fan. A youthful Bob Kress was not to be deterred by the petty confines of thermodynamics, however, and carried out a spectacular experiment that resulted in a flame-throwing device which threatened to destroy everything around it.

To return to basics, the low pressure rise does have its advantages, as there is no need to allow for the compressibility of air, thus simplifying the whole design process.

High school physics is all that is needed to calculate the thrust developed by a fan. Let us start with Sir Isaac Newton who realised that force (F) equals mass (m) multiplied by acceleration (a). That is

$$F = m.a \tag{1}$$

With the fan running, and the aircraft stationary on the ground, we can assume that the velocity of air outside the fan is zero but air is passing through the fan with velocity v.

Since $v = a.t$ where $t = $ time

then $F = \dfrac{m.v}{t} \tag{2}$

Now $F = T.g$ where 'T' is the static thrust and 'g' the acceleration due to gravity.

thus $T.g = \dfrac{m.v}{t} \tag{3}$

Also m/t is the mass flow, which equals the volume flow, Q, multiplied by the air density, d, thus

$$T.g = Q.d.v \tag{4}$$

The horsepower utilized in propelling air through the fan, P_a, is proportional to the volume flow multiplied by the air pressure, rise p.

$P_a = Q.p.k_1$ where k_1 is a constant

Also $P_a = T.v.k_2$ where k_2 is a constant

Substituting for Q and v in equation (4) gives:

$$T^2 = \frac{P_a^2.d}{p.k_1.k_2.g} \tag{5}$$

but $p = \dfrac{4.T}{\pi.D^2}$ where D is the diameter of the fan outlet

thus $T^3 = \dfrac{d.\pi. P_a^2.D^2}{4. k_1.k_2.g}$

or $T = \left[\dfrac{d.\pi}{4.k_1.k_2.g} \right]^{1/3} (P_a.D)^{2/3}$

$\qquad\qquad = 13 (P_a.D)^{2/3}$ if thrust is measured in pounds, P_a in horsepower and D in feet.

Finally, if P is the horsepower generated by the engine and E is the efficiency of the fan, then $E = P_a/P$

Therefore $T = \underline{13\,(E.\,P\,.\,D)}^{2/3}$ (6)

    All that mathematics may have seemed like heavy going, but it was worth the effort as equation (6) contains some very useful information. Firstly, thrust depends upon fan efficiency, engine horsepower and fan outlet diameter *and nothing else.* The fan efficiency must lie between 0 and 1 (or 0% and 100%). Let us take 0.5 as an example. If the horsepower is 2 bhp and the fan outlet diameter is 3 inches (0.25 feet) then the static thrust is

$$
\begin{aligned}
T &= 13\,(0.5 \times 2 \times 0.25)^{2/3} \\
  &= 13 \times 0.25^{2/3} \\
  &= 13 \times 0.40 \\
  &= 5.1 \text{ pounds}
\end{aligned}
$$

If we first increase the horsepower from 2 to 3 bhp then the thrust increases to 6.7 pounds. Similarly, if the efficiency is then increased from .5 to .75 (i.e. 50% to 75%) the thrust increases further to 8.8 pounds. Finally, if the fan outlet diameter is then increased from 3 to 4.5 inches the thrust increases further still to 11.6 pounds. Thus the combined effect of these increases in efficiency, horsepower, and diameter is to raise the thrust by a factor of 2.3.

    Let us take a closer look at each factor in turn:

Fan outlet diameter D If the fan diameter is made very large, this clearly requires a large airframe to contain it, hence the overall weight of the structure increases and the all important thrust-to-weight ratio may actually decrease. If the diameter is decreased, however, then the rpm required may be beyond the capability of most modern engines unless a heavy and cumbersome gearing unit is used. A compromise is therefore required, and this is determined by very practical considerations relating to availability of suitable engines and impeller manufacturing difficulties. For those reasons, most commercial ducted fan diameters lie in the remarkably narrow range of 4 to 6 inches.

    A word now about tailpipe outlet diameter. This is, strictly speaking, a feature of the airframe rather than the fan unit, but it can be considered to be an extension of the fan itself. If the tailpipe converges to a smaller diameter, D_t, than the fan outlet diameter, *static* thrust is lost. The effect can be calculated by substituting D_t for D in equation (6). Interestingly, however, the *dynamic* thrust (which is the thrust generated by the fan when the model is flying) will actually

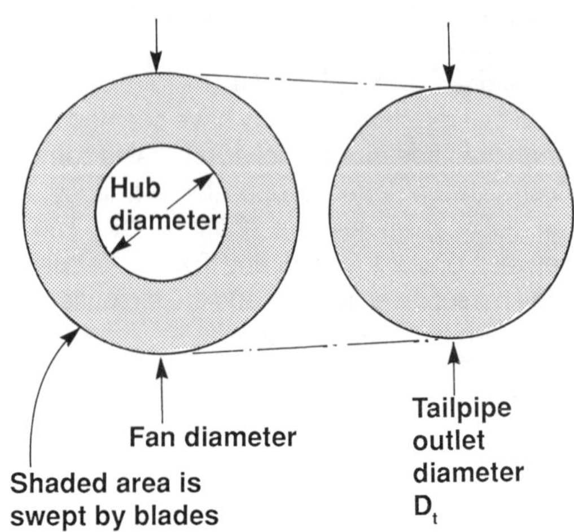

Fig. 2.3. The relationships between fan and tailpipe diameters. For 'zero contraction' conditions the shaded areas should be equal.

increase. This is of little use, however, if there is insufficient static thrust to get the aircraft off the ground or to pull it through vertical manoeuvres. There is a clear case here for variable geometry tailpipes just like certain full size jets utilize. A commonly used, practical compromise is to adopt a 'zero contraction' tailpipe where the tailpipe outlet area is equal to the area swept by the fan blades which equates to the area of the fan less the area of the impeller hub. This gives a tailpipe diameter which is roughly 90% of the fan diameter for most commercial units (Fig. 2.3).

Fan efficiency E Equation (6) can also be used in reverse to calculate efficiency, provided that the engine horsepower and fan diameter are known and that the thrust can be measured. A simple spring balance gives a rough indication of thrust, T. More sophisticated methods will be mentioned later. Efficiencies calculated in this way give values of around 25% for the earliest twisted aluminium sheet fans using 0.5 to 1.0 cc engines. Fan diameters were typically 3 to 4 inches diameter with measured thrusts ranging from ¼ to ½ pound. The later impellers fabricated from fibre and reinforced nylon typical of the early commercial units gave efficiencies around 60%.

The third generation fans exemplified by the VIOJETT and DYNAMAX fans have now reached 80% efficiency and seem incapable of further significant improvement.

Equation (6) can also be used to provide a simple test of a fan manufacturer's claims. If the advertisement suggests that 18 pounds of thrust may be obtained from a 5 inch diameter fan using a 3 bhp

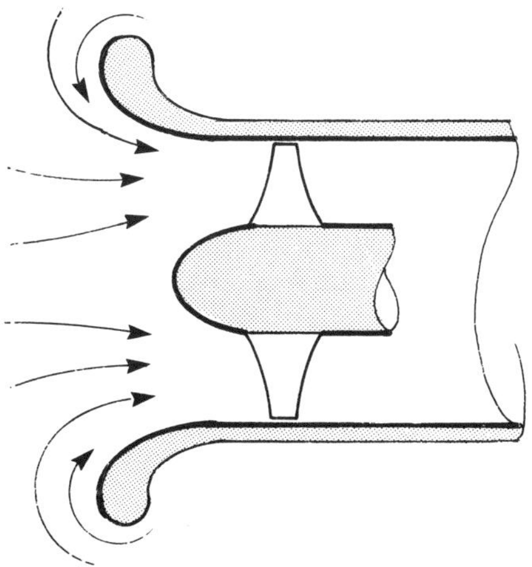

engine, it is a simple matter to calculate the efficiency of the fan unit. If this exceeds 100% (128% in the example quoted) you can be quite sure that it is the manufacturer who is wrong, *not* Sir Isaac Newton!

Where do the efficiency losses come from? First of all, it should be understood that efficiencies derived from equation (6) assume no inlet loss. This implies the use of a perfect bellmouth inlet (Fig. 2.4) which can gather air from all around the fan. If, under these conditions, the derived efficiency is, say 70%, then a 30% loss of efficiency must be accounted for. Bob Kress produced the following "inventory" of losses for one of his fans:

Impeller losses:

Friction in impeller annulus	7.0%	
Blade root and tip losses	6.9%	
Blade profile drag losses	6.7%	
Sub total		20.6%

Stator losses:	4.5%
Duct loss due to friction drag:	1.5%
Drag associated with the engine:	3.5%
TOTAL	30.1%

The magnitude of each item of lost efficiency is critically dependent on fan design. Bob Violett claims that he has managed to reduce the total losses to 15%. A notable feature of the VIOJETT design is the 'constant area-ruling' concept. This is intended to minimise the drag that derives from the many pressure changes that occur as air passes through the fan. If, for example, the fan shroud diameter is the same along the length of the fan from inlet to outlet (i.e. a perfect cylinder),

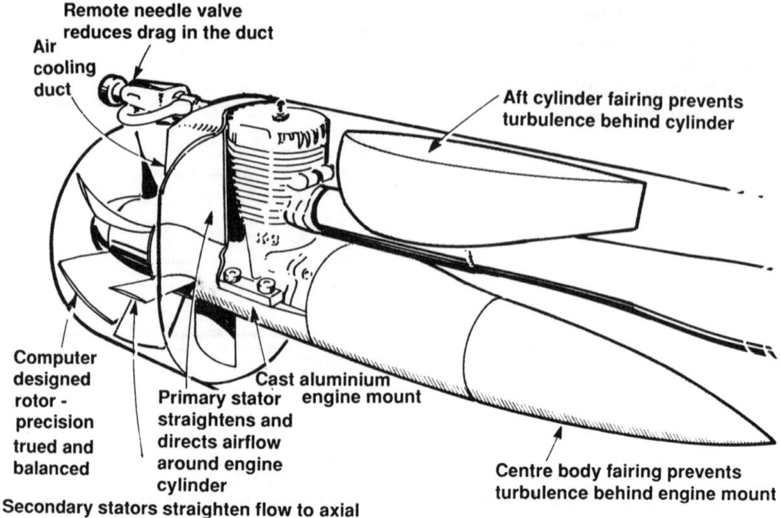

Fig. 2.5. VIOJETT cutaway, showing use of fairings and duct shape changes to provide 'constant area ruling.'

then the pressure is forced to drop as the incoming air meets the spinner and is obliged to pass around it and the fan centrebody. An additional pressure decrease occurs when the engine is reached, as this further reduces the effective area of the duct. The duct area suddenly increases as the air passes the engine, thus the pressure rises. Further pressure changes occur as the air flows past the tuned pipe.

Each pressure change results in an air velocity change and (generally) in the formation of eddys where energy is converted from motion into heat and therefore lost as far as thrust is concerned. Violett seeks to minimize this effect by changing the shape of the shroud or duct so that the effective cross-sectional area of the duct through which air can pass remains constant. He also deploys fairings around the cylinder head, tuned pipe and centre body to achieve the same effect (Fig. 2.5). The fairings have a secondary benefit, in that they have aerodynamic shapes which smooth (or streamline) the flow of air thus minimizing flow separation which would otherwise lead to eddy formation.

An understanding of the use of fairings and the constant area ruling concept is important not only to the design of fans but also to the design of inlet and outlet ducts, and any intrusions into them to accommodate retracts, servos, fuel tanks etc.

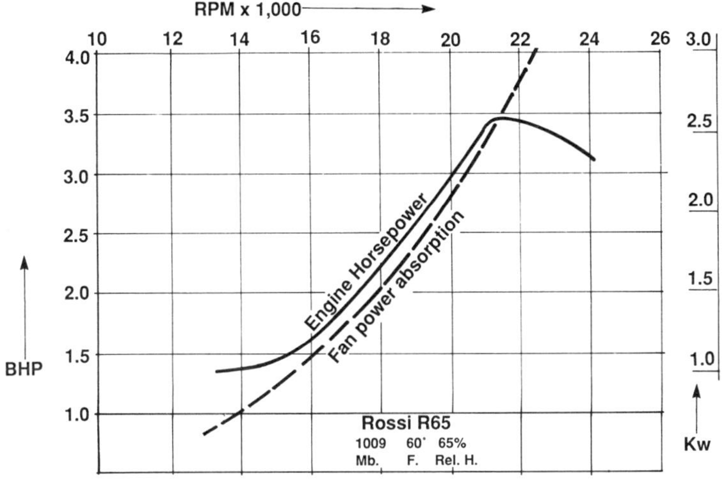

Fig. 2.6. Curve showing relationship between horsepower and rpm for a ROSSI-65 engine fitted with a quiet pipe. Also shown is the curve relating power absorbed, to rpm, for a BOSS 602 fan unit.

Engine horsepower P The selection of a suitable value of P to put in equation (6) should be treated with care. Indiscriminate use of the manufacturer's figures could give rise to calculated values of thrust or efficiency that could be misleading. What is really needed is a graph relating horsepower P to engine rpm, ideally for the same fuel, tuned pipe, pipe length and atmospheric conditions that are used when testing the fan. In practice the graphs produced by engine experts such as Peter Chinn and Mike Billinton, which are published in many aeromodelling magazines around the world, can be used, with minor adjustments, to account for the different conditions mentioned above. (Fig. 2.6) shows just such a graph obtained by Mike Billinton for a Rossi 65 ducted fan engine. Also shown in Fig. 2.6 is the power absorption curve for the BOSS 602 ducted fan. Where the two curves intersect gives the rpm at which the fan will run when driven by a Rossi 65 under those conditions. The engine horsepower at that rpm can also be read from the curve. This horsepower value can then be used in equation (6) to calculate the static thrust we might expect to achieve from that combination of fan and engine.

Fig. 2.6 is fundamental to understanding the performance of ducted fans, especially if used in conjunction with equation (6). It shows quite clearly that fan and engine need to be carefully matched. Ideally the cross-over point for the curves should occur near to the

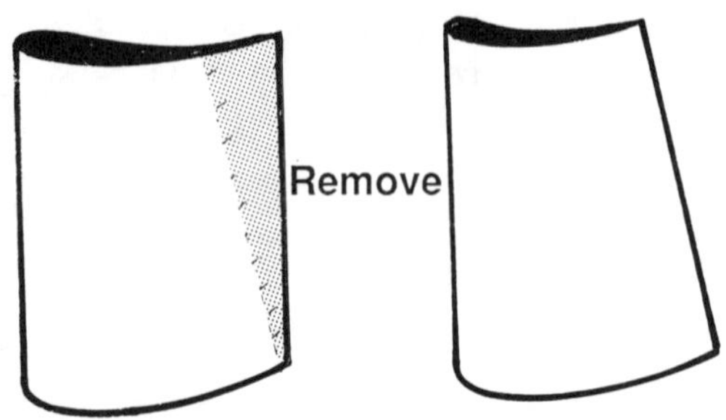

Fig. 2.7. Blade reprofiling can increase rpm and hence allow the engine to operate closer to its peak horsepower thereby delivering more thrust.

peak in the engine horsepower curve, preferably slightly towards the lower rpm side of the peak so that the fan will unload in flight, thus allowing the operating point to move up to the peak horsepower. Both curves are adjustable to a certain extent. Changes in tuned pipe length can move the peak horsepower to lower or higher rpm and changes to the fuel (nitromethane content particularly) will move the peak to higher or lower horsepower values. If we are prepared to take a file or saw to the impeller we can, for instance, reduce the chord of each blade. The best approach is to leave the root chord unchanged and gradually taper the blade towards the tip, by removing material from the *trailing edge* (Fig. 2.7). It will be necessary to clean up and reprofile the blades, and even then fan efficiency will probably decrease. Hopefully, of course, this loss will be more than offset by allowing the fan to absorb more horsepower by rotating faster and moving up the horsepower curve. This is precisely what Colonel Bob Thacker did to his BYROJET fan to gain 400 rpm and ½ pound of thrust. Such drastic measures are not for everyone, as there is always the possibility that they could make matters worse.

A more elegant solution is to design an impeller that can be adjusted at will. The British company SLEC produces a variable pitch fan and an American company has recently introduced the HURRICANE fan which allows the number of blades to be varied. This is also a feature of the BOSS fans, which can operate with 12, 10, 9, 8, 6 and 3, or 2 blades, although choice is usually restricted to the higher numbers. In no case should the fan be allowed to exceed 25,000 rpm. We have also been doing some experiments recently with the MICROMOLD impellers. By machining the angle of the blade root segments it is possible to vary blade numbers from 5 to 8 and thereby 'match' the impeller to a number of engines of different horsepower. As with all such experiments, it is absolutely essential to understand the risks involved with such modifications as the manufacturer's guarantee and liability will almost certainly be in-

Fig. 2.8. Blading modifications to MICROMOLD impellers. The 5-bladed fan is normal but 6, 7 and 8 (shown here) bladed versions are available.

validated. Blade integrity and retention is vitally important: to this end Turbofan replaces front and back plates supplied with the MICRO-MOLD impeller by machined aluminium alloy plates (Fig. 2.8).

Having dealt in some depth with the importance of equation (6), it is worth exploring the usefulness of some of the equations that preceded it.

Fan pressure rise, p Referring back to the derivation of equation (6) reveals the relationship

$$p = \frac{4T}{\pi D^2}$$

If we choose values of $T = 10$ pounds and $D = 3.6$ inches which are typical, say, of a VIOJETT fan in a Sportshark airframe, we then calculate that p is approximately equal to one pound per square inch (1 psi). This may not sound very much but it compares in magnitude to the pressure rise inside a typical tuned pipe. It is, therefore, quite possible to tap pressure from the rear duct to pressurise the fuel tanks. The vertical head of fuel that could be pumped would exceed 2 feet. This arrangement avoids the use of long lengths of pressure tubing flapping around inside the rear duct. Its only disadvantage is that any dust or dirt entering the rear duct might find its way along the pressure line and into the fuel tank. A friend could find no other way to explain the presence of finely-chopped grass in his fuel filter!

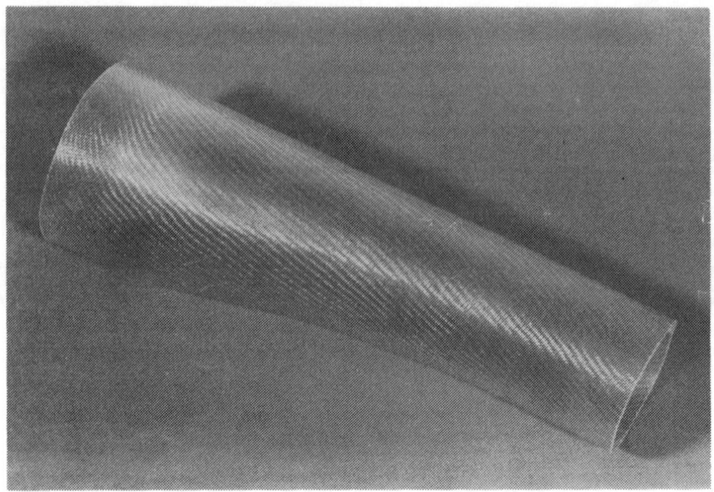

Fig. 2.9. The inlet duct is susceptible to collapsing under negative pressures. It must therefore be much stiffer than the outlet duct. This duct was made from two layers of relatively heavy glass cloth.

Another aspect of the pressure rise is that the ducts should be capable of withstanding the pressure drop across them. This is usually no problem for the outlet duct provided that its seam joint is sound, but the inlet duct can experience a pressure *reduction* (especially if there are no cheat inlets) and may collapse if it is under-designed. For instance, the load tending to collapse the inlet duct in my MiG-15 exceeds 100 pounds applied uniformly over its surface area. The critical load to cause collapse depends primarily on the stiffness of duct material, rather than its strength. Fortunately, a considerable increase in stiffness can be provided by epoxying carbon fibre cord around the duct, without increasing the weight significantly. Alternatively, the duct must be made from heavier glass cloth (Fig. 2.9).

Velocity of air passing through the fan outlet. v

Another equation referred to in the derivation of thrust was: $P_a = T.v.k_2$ where $k_2 = 1/550$. This may be rearranged to give

$$v = \frac{550 \text{ E.P}}{T}$$

Taking typical values for the VIOJETT in a Sportshark airframe ($E = 0.80$, $P = 3.8$ bhp and $T = 10$ pounds) gives

$$v = 167 \text{ feet per second}$$
$$= 114 \text{ mph}$$

This relates to the static condition with the aircraft stationary on the ground. In flight the speed of the aircraft will increase until the reducing dynamic thrust is just balanced by the increasing drag of the aircraft. This corresponds, very approximately, to a thrust of 5 pounds as we shall see later. Changes in horsepower and efficiency are relatively small and tend to balance each other. Thus we can calculate the velocity of air through the fan outlet to be about 230 mph with the aircraft travelling at approximately 155 mph. Anyone having stuck their hand out of a car window at 70 mph will appreciate that any items inside the duct will need to be secured very thoroughly!

2.3 Fan design

Having wrung, it would seem, the last drop of usefulness from equation (6) let us now consider its limitations. It has already been shown that it tells us nothing about dynamic thrust, nor does it show how to *design* a fan — only what we can expect from it. Both subjects are beyond the scope of this book, but a brief indication of what steps are involved in fan design might be worthwhile. The process is roughly as follows:

1) Decide what engine is to be used and hence the available horsepower, also the desired fan diameter, then change the form of equation (6) to include dimensionless fan characteristics Ψ(flow) ν (pressure).

2) Estimate the efficiency, E and solve the equations for Ψ and ν.

3) These values of Ψ and ν can then be used to calculate *rotor* flow angles and swirl velocities.

4) Lift coefficients and solidity ratios can then be calculated at different positions along the length of the blade so as to achieve the desired fan characteristics $\Psi\nu$. This effectively determines the number of blades, their chords and profile, by taking into account appropriate manufacturing limitations.

5) Knowing the lift coefficient allows the airfoil of the blade to be selected and this then determines the angle of attack (or pitch) of the blade.

6) Steps 4) and 5) are repeated for the stator blades with the objective of eliminating swirl in the airstream leaving the fan (Fig. 2.10).

7) Re-estimate the efficiency based on the calculated impeller and stator blade configurations and reiterate steps 3), 4), 5) and 6) if necessary.

8) Calculate the static thrust and decide if it is adequate before producing engineering drawings for the manufacture of the fan. If the thrust is not adequate, then the designer must look once more at equation (6) to see whether he can increase the diameter,

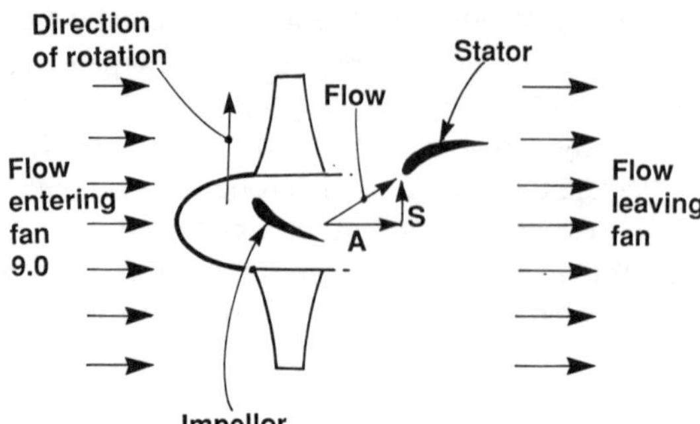

Fig. 2.10. How the air flow leaving the impeller has an axial component 'A' and rotational or swirl component 'S'. The swirl should be removed by the stator blades which convert it back into axial flow.

horsepower or efficiency of the fan.

The whole process is quite complicated and time consuming, and obviously benefits from the application of computer-aided design techniques. Nevertheless, some important messages emerge from the exercise.

Impeller rpm

Firstly, thrust is proportional to $(rpm)^2$. Thus, if thrust is measured and the rpm of the fan noted, then the thrust can be calculated for any other rpm since

$$T = (rpm)^2 \times constant \tag{7}$$

This is quite useful, as rpm can be measured much more easily and accurately than thrust so we now have a way of estimating how thrust (and therefore the performance of our aircraft) is likely to change if we change the engine, fuel, pipe, pipe length, carburettor choke size, throttle setting, fuel pump, impeller, blade shape, etc. etc. This presupposes, of course, that we do not change the general installation (duct diameter, length, inlet shape) at the same time. Fig. 3.13 (page 56) shows a typical plot of thrust versus rpm.

Stator efficiency

The stator fulfills two functions. The first is structural in that it usually supports the fan centrebody to which the engine is attached. The second function is that it serves to straighten the air flow and recover some of the swirl energy. This is only achieved at the expense of increased drag, however, which may exceed the recovered swirl energy if the designer is not extremely careful. The swirl energy loss is roughly proportional to the square root of the swirl angle which is in turn related to the solidity ratio. Solidity is the blade width at half its

Fig. 2.11. The impellers having a range of solidity ratios. (a) BOSS 602 (b) RK 740 (c) Home-made fan by Marcus Norman (the forerunner of the MICROMOLD impeller). (d) RK 049 (e) RK 40 (f) MICROMOLD

length multiplied by the number of blades, divided by the circumference at half the blade length. In other words it approximates to the proportion of blade swept area occupied by the blades when viewed from the front of the fan. The BOSS 602 has a high solidity ratio of 0.75 due primarily to having 12 blades. The Micromold fan, having only 5 blades, has a solidity radio of 0.44. A low solidity impeller typified by the Micromold fan gives a swirl energy loss of around 10% if left unrecovered by the stators, whereas the swirl energy loss of the BOSS 602 fan is as high as 30%, a figure I have confirmed by undertaking thrust tests using a BOSS 602 fan with and without stator blades fitted. Figure 2.11 shows a variety of impellers having different solidities.

Dynamic thrust

We keep returning to this rather tantalising subject without, it seems, making much progress. In the case of a simple propeller, the pylon race enthusiast must decide on a compromise between a high pitch blade, which will give excellent thrust at high air speeds but may be stalled when the aircraft is stationary, and a low pitch prop which will give the highest static thrust but disappointing top end performance. The compromise is drawn, usually by experience, but the nature of

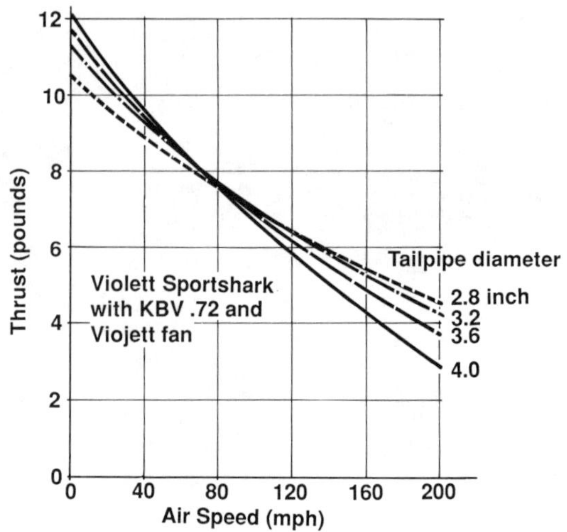

Fig. 2.12. The effect of tailpipe diameter on static and dynamic thrust. (*courtesy Bob Violett*)

the deal should be clear: a racing machine must have good acceleration as well as a high maximum speed.

It is unlikely that ducted fan propelled aircraft will ever compete effectively with propeller driven models when it comes to pylon racing due to their relatively large weight, size and drag penalties. In some respects, however, fans have a few advantages over the propeller insofar as the static versus dynamic thrust compromise is concerned. Not only does the fan designer have the capability of changing impeller blade pitch (as for the propeller) but he can also achieve much the same effect by changing stator blade angles and tailpipe outlet diameter. If the stator blade pitch is adjusted to remove *all* the swirl under static conditions, then at high speed the stator will be imparting a *negative* swirl to the flow, thus reducing efficiency and dynamic thrust. Therefore it is best not to eliminate all the swirl when the aircraft is stationary. Similarly with the tailpipe: zero contraction may well give maximum static thrust but, by reducing the diameter a bit further, higher dynamic thrust can be achieved. (Fig. 2.12).

Thus the fan designer can, in a sense, have the best of both worlds by a carefully selected combination of rotor blade pitch, stator blade pitch and tailpipe size, so that high efficiency is maintained throughout the speed range and the blades never stall no matter where the aircraft is in the flight envelope.

A word of caution is due at this point. If the impeller blades are allowed to stall for whatever reason (too great a pitch or too small a tailpipe) the fan will no longer absorb the engine horsepower and the engine may then overspeed with obviously serious results. Therefore,

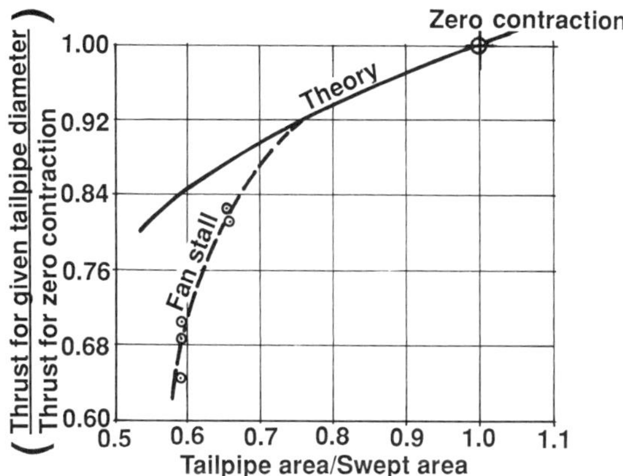

Fig. 2.13. Effect of tailpipe diameter on thrust showing the effect of blade stall (*courtesy Bob Kress*)

be warned if you are tempted to experiment in this area! Fig. 2.13, which is derived from equation (6), shows how thrust is affected when the fan is forced to stall by contracting the tailpipe too far.

Blade tip losses

Lost efficiency due to clearances between the tip of the blade and the inner surface of the fan shroud occurs due to increased vortex shedding at the blade tip, increased radial flow along the blade and reduced pressure rise across the fan, due to air leaking back from the high to the low pressure side of the fan. The last of these three factors is of overwhelming importance in full-size compressor design. Because the ducted fan is a low pressure rise device, the effect is less drastic but can still account for considerable losses. Figure 2.14 is derived for a high solidity fan of 4.5 inch diameter. Maximum measured thrust (9.92 pounds) corresponds to a stationary blade clearance of .030 inches (0.75 mm). Any attempt to reduce the clearance results in the blade tips rubbing, due to the combined effects of vibration and stretching of the blades under centrifugal forces. It is assumed that the minimum practical blade tip clearance at full rpm is .010 inches (i.e. the blade stretches .020 inches). Allowing the stationary clearance to increase to .125 inches (3 mm) will reduce the thrust from 9.92 pounds to 8.65 pounds (i.e. by 13%). This is an exceptionally large clearance; most fans should show typical clearances of half this value which would reduce the thrust from 9.92 to 9.45 pounds (5%). There is, therefore, every incentive to centre the impeller properly in the first place and minimize vibration.

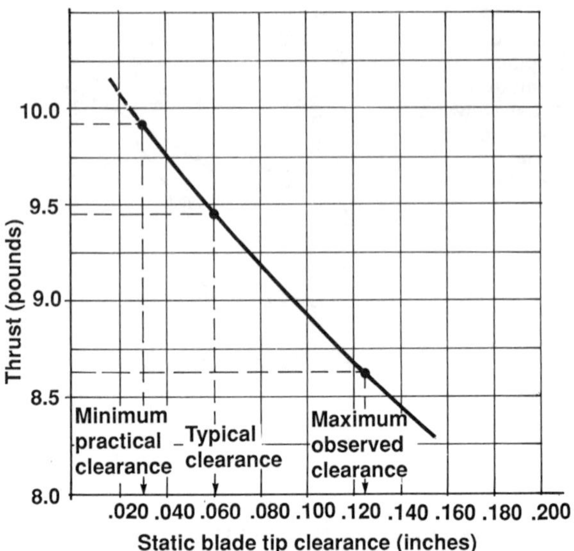

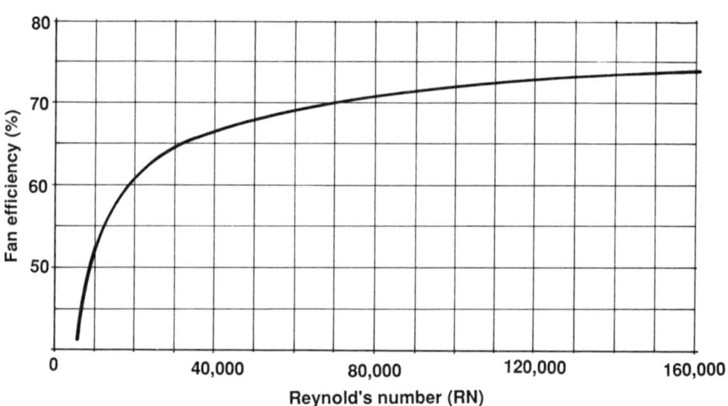

Fig. 2.15. Effect of Reynolds number (RN) on impeller efficiency (*courtesy Bob Kress*)

Reynolds Number (RN) effects

Impeller efficiency is directly related to drag losses arising from the blades themselves. These effects are much more severe if the blade tip is operating at Reynolds Numbers below RN = 40,000 (Fig. 2.15).

Reynolds Number can be calculated quite simply for a fan blade using the following equation:-

$$RN = 4.624 \text{ (rpm) C.R.} \tag{8}$$

where C is the blade tip chord in inches, and R is the impeller radius at the blade tip (also in inches). Thus for a 6 inch diameter fan rotating at 20,000 rpm with a blade tip chord of 1 inch we can calculate a Reynolds Number RN = 277,000. This is way off the graph drawn in Fig. 2.15 but obviously corresponds to a relatively high efficiency around 80%.

At the other end of the spectrum a small impeller of, say, 3 inches diameter turning at 20,000 rpm with a blade tip chord of 0.5 inches would give RN = 69,000. This has brought the impeller efficiency down to about 70%. Any further reduction in fan size without a corresponding increase in rpm would clearly have disastrous consequences for efficiency. Remember, also, that impeller drag is only one contribution to lost efficiency. There are other factors that also become more important as the size decreases; a blade tip clearance of, for example, .120 inch (3 mm) would be more severe for a 3 inch fan than for the 4.5 inch fan for which Fig. 2.14 is derived.

Effect of atmospheric conditions

Variations in temperature, pressure and humidity can all have a significant effect on the thrust put out by a fan. Not only does engine performance vary, but so does fan efficiency due to changes in air density. Typically, we might expect thrust to drop by around 15% as temperature is raised from 20°F to 100°F at constant barometric pressure. If the pressure was to suddenly drop, or we could be elevated from sea level to an altitude of 5,000 feet without any change in temperature, then thrust would drop by around 18%. A reduction in humidity would also reduce thrust. The effects are made more severe because the aircraft's wings will also provide less lift as temperature rises and humidity and pressure decrease.

We conclude that the high desert is no place for a ducted fan. However, if you are fortunate enough to be flying in freezing fog in the Bering Straits, those vertical rolls could be quite spectacular!

Fig. 2.16. Master of the mini-fan, Alec Cornish-Trestrail, poses with two of his latest creations, both driven by twin RK-720 fan units. Note the tiny impeller which packs enough punch to power both the MiG-29 Fulcrum (*top*) and F-15 Eagle (*bottom*)

3 THE DUCTED FAN UNIT

3.1 Manufacturing considerations

Chapter 2 showed how to design a fan and calculate the thrust that might be expected from it, but it said very little about the way the fan should be manufactured. The design process has to take into account what the manufacturing options are likely to be with regard to dimensional tolerances, materials selection, production techniques and cost. We have already seen how the designer has to compromise between the desirability of squeezing even more horsepower into smaller and smaller fans, and the decrease in efficiency that is its inevitable consequence. Well, more compromises will now be discussed.

3.2 Materials technology

The most critical component in a ducted fan unit is the impeller blade. This represents the cutting edge of fan technology. The blade must withstand the very large centrifugal and bending stresses placed upon it without breaking or distorting significantly. Distortion is important because the efficiency of the fan depends upon the blade keeping the precise aerodynamic shape that the designer intended. Blade failure is obviously undesirable as the rotor will become unbalanced leading to more blade damage and even destruction of the engine. More importantly, flying blades are extremely dangerous to anyone in their path. Materials possessing very high strength and stiffness are therefore needed and they should also be light (low density), as this has the double benefit of reducing centrifugal forces as well as the overall weight of the fan.

Early use of twisted aluminium sheet blades quickly led to fatigue failures and did not allow accurate reproduction of desirable airfoils.

Later experiments with fibrous materials and plastics, notably nylon and polycarbonate, were quite successful, but it was not until the plastics were reinforced with glass fibre that the full power of modern racing engines could be harnessed effectively. Nowadays the impellers of certain commercial fans are fabricated from nylon reinforced by carbon fibres. These space-age fibres have the highest specific stiffness known to man and are, not surprisingly, very expensive. They are also well suited to injection moulding techniques which allow the blades to be manufactured to very close tolerances on a mass-production basis. The same materials are also used for the shroud (which cannot be allowed to distort otherwise large tip clearances would result) and for the stator blades (which often have to support the weight and torque of the engine). With some designs, the engine is even bolted onto fibre reinforced plastics though most manufacturers prefer to use cast and machined aluminium alloys for this application. Aluminium alloys are also used for the impeller blade retention system in certain commercial units.

3.3 Commercial Ducted Fan Units

Table 3.1 lists all currently available ducted fan units known to the author. A brief description of each unit follows. Manufacturers' addresses, from whence further information can be obtained, are listed in Appendix 1.

Aerojet 25 Fan

Supplier: Southeast Model Products This is a conventional tractor unit developed by Larry Epifiano from one of the earliest commercial units:- the AXIFLO RK20B designed by Bob Kress. There have been no significant dimensional changes but the new unit features a Lexan/glass rotor, spinner and engine mount. These improvements enable it to harness the power of the new K&B .28 engine which, it is hoped, will shortly be available. The manufacturer claims that this fan/engine combination should yield 4½ pounds of thrust. It is also suited to the OS-25 DF engine. Although the impeller is a single piece injection moulding some assembly is required. Two rows of stator blades are featured; one row in front and one behind the engine. The size and shape of the unit make it ideally suited to a podded, or nacelle, type of installation, especially if one of the special foam inlets available from Kress Jets is used, (Fig. 3.1). The fan also features an integral 6 ounce fuel tank which doubles as a streamlined aft centre-body fairing. Starting is achieved by a simple cone starter which engages the spinner as for a normal propeller driven model.

TABLE 3.1 COMMERCIALLY AVAILABLE DUCTED FAN UNITS

	ENGINE cu. in.	IMPELLER DIAMETER inches	No. BLADES	MANUFACTURER/SUPPLIER
AEROJET 25	.21/25	4.2	5	South East Model Products USA
BAUER BM 40/81	.40/.81	4.9	6 pusher	H.R. Modelltechnik, West Germany
BAEUR BM61-91/81	.61/.90	5.4	6 pusher	" " " "
BOSS PRO	.61/.81	5.2	12	Lyco, Sweden
BYROJET	.61/.90	6.0	5 pusher	Byron Originals, USA
DYNAMAX	.61/.77	4.8	11	Jet Model Products, USA
FORCE AIR I	.77/.81	5.2	5 x 2	Force Air, USA
GLEICHAUF	.65/.90	6.0	6 pusher	Rolfe Gleichauf, West Germany
HURRICANE 4")		4.0	5-8 pusher	Korney,USA
HURRICANE 5")	.40/.90	5.0	or tractor	" "
HURRICANE 6")		6.0		" "
JET AGE 5"	.45/.81	5.0	8	Jet Age Model Aircraft Co., USA
JET AGE 6"	.81/.90	6.0	9	" " " " "
MICROMOLD	.40/.45	4.9	5	Micromold UK
RK-720 MkII	.20/.25	3.4	7	Kress Jets, USA
RK-740 MkIII	.40/.45	4.2	7	" " "
THORJET	.40/.45	4.9	5	Thorpe Brothers, UK
TURBAX I	.40/.45	4.8	5	Jet Hanger Hobbies, USA
TURBAX III	.61/.65	4.8	5	" " " "
VIOJETT	.72/.77	4.6	7	Bob Violett Models, USA

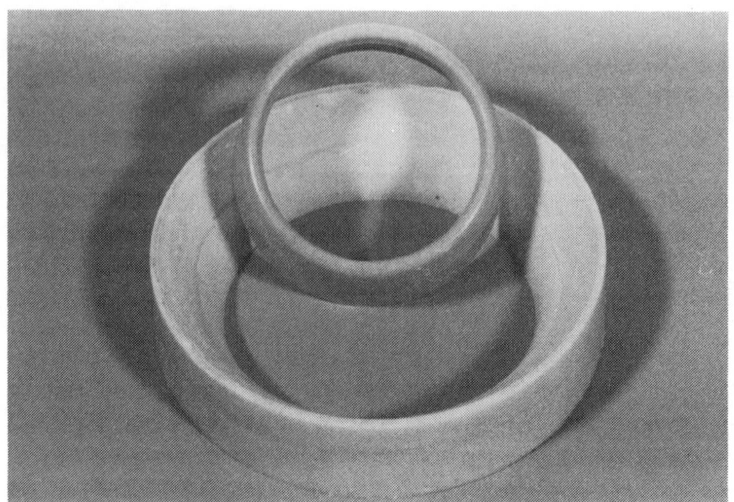

Fig. 3.1. Specially shaped foam inlets for the RK20B/AEROJET25 fan and the BOSS 602 fan units yield high thrusts and suit nacelle, or pod, type installations.

Bauer BM 40/81 and BM 61-91/81 Fans

Suppliers: H. R. Modelltechnik, Both fans are pushers and were originally designed for use with standard sports type engines which deliver peak horsepower in the range 14,000 to 16,000 rpm (Fig. 1.9). The biggest of the two fans is one of the heaviest ducted fan units currently available (outside diameter 6.9 inches, weight 19 ounces). Two centrebody fairings are provided, one for the inlet and a longer projection for the outlet, through which an electric starter is inserted. The arrangement is ideally suited to a front induction, side exhaust engine. In recent years both the smaller and the larger versions have shown that they can absorb the power of engines up to .81 and .91 cubic inches respectively. A considerable amount of assembly is required (Fig. 3.2). The manufacturer claims 4½ pound thrust at 14,000 rpm for the BM40/81 and 8 pound thrust at 14,600 rpm for the BM 61-91/81. Presumably much larger thrusts would be generated with more powerful engines, as the larger fan, for example, is absorbing only 2 BHP at 14,600 rpm.

Boss Pro Fan

Supplier: K.B. Lyco The BOSS 601 was the first commercial fan unit manufactured in continental Europe. As engine horsepower has increased so has the fan been developed, firstly to the BOSS 602 version in 1982 and now the BOSS PRO which is suited to the most

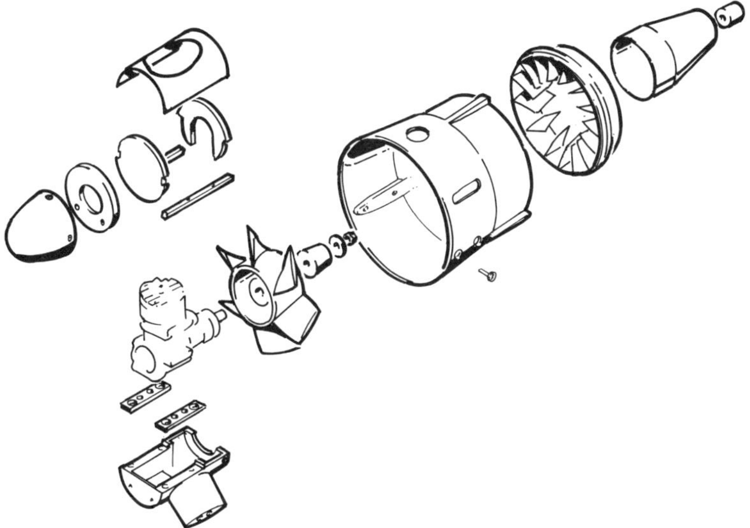

Fig. 3.2. Exploded diagram of BAUER fan.

Fig. 3.3. The BOSS PRO fan in the 'pusher' configuration. (Fig. 1.8 shows the more normal tractor arrangement)

powerful .80 size engines (Fig. 3.3). It has a very high solidity impeller which can be modified to match the horsepower of a range of engines by removing 2, 3, 4, or 6 blades in such a way that impeller symmetry and balance is maintained. There is a fair amount of work involved in assembling the fan.

The BOSS PRO resembles the original BOSS 601 only insofar as the external dimensions and blade geometry are concerned. Virtually all the materials have changed (carbon fibre is used in rotating parts) and the blade retention system is new. The rotor hub is sleeved to give accurate alignment and ease of balancing, but most importantly, the stator blade and front bearing support system is completely redesigned. An aluminium spool is attached to the front bearing housing of the engine. The spool is then slipped into the centre aluminium ring on the stator blade assembly. This ensures that the impeller is located centrally inside the shroud with minimum blade tip clearance. It also provides a second point of support for the engine (in addition to the normal mounting lugs), and thus strengthens the entire structure and cuts down vibration.

The BOSS PRO is quite a flexible unit in that it can also serve as a pusher fan provided the direction of rotation of the engine is reversed. This is facilitated by separate mounting systems for the fan unit and the engine. Starting is achieved either with a belt or a conventional cone starter on the spinner. A specially contoured foam inlet can be supplied, (Fig. 3.1) if a podded installation is required. In this form, using a Rossi 81 at 20,000 rpm, 11 pounds of thrust should be produced provided an outlet diameter of 4.5 inches is used. Smaller tailpipe diameters than 4 inches may cause the blades to stall.

Byrojet Fan
Supplier: Byron Originals This is a simple, rugged unit that has sold well around the world for many years (Fig. 1.10). There does not seem to have been any significant change to the design since it was first introduced, yet it is still capable of handling the most powerful ducted fan engines available. The manufacturer claims in excess of 13 pounds of thrust using a Rossi-90 engine at 20,400 rpm.

The fan unit is a pusher type of relatively large dimensions (7.5 inches outside diameter across the 'bellmouth' inlet lip). It requires a special tuned pipe that returns the exhaust gases through the fan and thence out of the tailpipe (Fig. 3.4). It can only be started by means of an electric starter with an extension which engages the rotor via the tailpipe. There is virtually no assembly work to do and the manufacturer recommends that no attempt should be made to balance the impeller, as manufacturing tolerances ensure that this is not necessary. The fan is designed for bulkhead mounting.

The relatively large size of the fan limits its use to larger airframes typical of the nine kits designed for its use by Byron Originals. Even so, several other kit manufacturers and scratchbuilders have elected

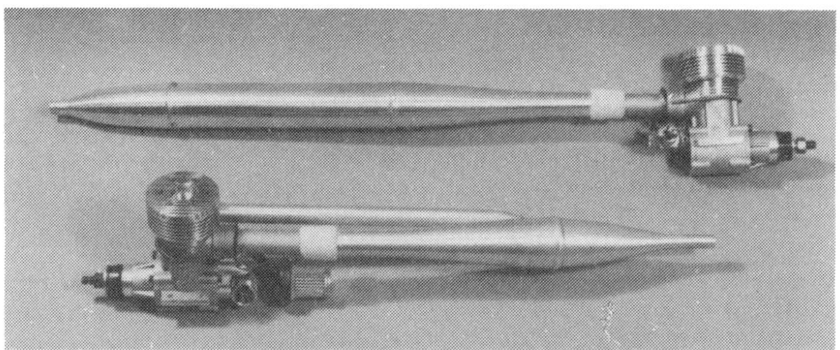

Fig. 3.4. Comparing a normal type of tuned pipe used for a tractor installation (*top*), with one designed for the BYROJET fan (*bottom*).

to use the BYROJET in their designs. It is usually necessary to enlarge the normal intake areas or provide a 'cheat' inlet. The pusher configuration is not as efficient as the normal tractor arrangement when it comes to directing air over the cylinder head, so engines with additional cooling fins (heat sink heads) are often used with the BYROJET. Alternatively, adequate cooling can usually be achieved by inverting the engine so that the cylinder head projects into a cheat inlet in the belly of the aircraft.

Dynamax Fan

Supplier: Jet Model Products Tom Cook is another American pioneer of the ducted fan movement. He broke new ground when his twin fan Phantom was placed first in the 1980 USA Scale Masters tournament. His search for more powerful and reliable fan/engine combinations led him to work with an aerodynamicist from General Electric to design a new fan of roughly the same dimensions as the popular Turbax I, yet permitting the use of larger engines like the Rossi 65 or OS77DF. This resulted in a high solidity impeller having 11 blades and 16 stator blades capable of producing 10 pounds of thrust at 22,000 rpm, (Fig. 3.5).

The fan is designed for beam (or rail) mounting and requires some assembly. The aluminium centrebody is drilled and tapped to suit the engine the purchaser selects. Starting is by a normal cone starter.

Tom has recently introduced the DYNAMAX II fan which includes some refinements to the original design.

Force Air I Fan

Supplier: Force Air Technology Inc. This somewhat controversial unit is unique among commercial fans, in that it utilizes twin impellers with three rows of stator blades set in a transparent plastic tubular shroud,

Fig. 3.5.(a) The
DYNAMAX fan
impeller.

3.5.(b) 'Exploded' view.

Fig. 3.6. The
GLEICHAUF
fan unit.

These additional components cause the unit to be rather heavy at 23 ounces but are presumably required to achieve the manufacturer's claimed 18 pounds thrust capability. In a recently published test on a FORCE AIR I fan installed in a Bob Parkinson Regal Eagle, the measured thrust was 4¼ pounds. This compared with 6½ pounds thrust for a BYROJET in a nearly identical airframe. In both cases the fans were driven by an OS77DF engine. Quite clearly the installation of both fans was far from ideal with considerable inlet and outlet losses. Also the thrust measurement was by a simple spring balance which could easily lead to errors. Nevertheless, both models flew quite well. Apparently, the fan unit is being redesigned with the objective of achieving the claimed thrust figures. It is not clear at the time of going to press, however, when the new units are likely to be available.

The FORCE AIR I is designed for beam mounting in a standard tractor configuration and can be started with a conventional cone starter.

Gleichauf fan
Supplier: Rolf Gleichauf Modellbautechnik This is another pusher design, somewhat similar to the BYROJET, in utilizing a 6 inch diameter impeller in a shroud with a bellmouth inlet (Fig. 3.6). The engine mount is conceptually similar to the BYROJET but uses four, rather than three, cantilevered supports. The GLEICHAUF fan is a hybrid in that it uses the stators and aft centrebody fairing of the BAUER fan. Also 'borrowed' from the BAUER fan is the impeller, which has six blades. This means that it is suited to engines that reach their peak horsepower at relatively low rpm. The Rossi-81 horsepower peaks around 22,000 rpm, but it will only turn the GLEICHAUF fan at 17,000 rpm at which its horsepower is limited to 3.25 bhp (Fig. 3.7). However, if the same engine is converted to a diesel using the Davies Diesel Developments (USA) kit, the rpm increases to 18,000, and 13 pounds of thrust is generated. A remarkable feature of all diesels is their fuel economy. This is particularly true of simple two-stroke engines. The dieselized Rossi 81 needs only 10 ounces of fuel for a 10 minute flight compared with 20-24 ounces for the usual glow version. The diesel should also run a little quieter and cooler.

Hurricane Fans
Supplier: Steve Korney This is another new name among ducted fan manufacturers. With very little information to go on at the time of

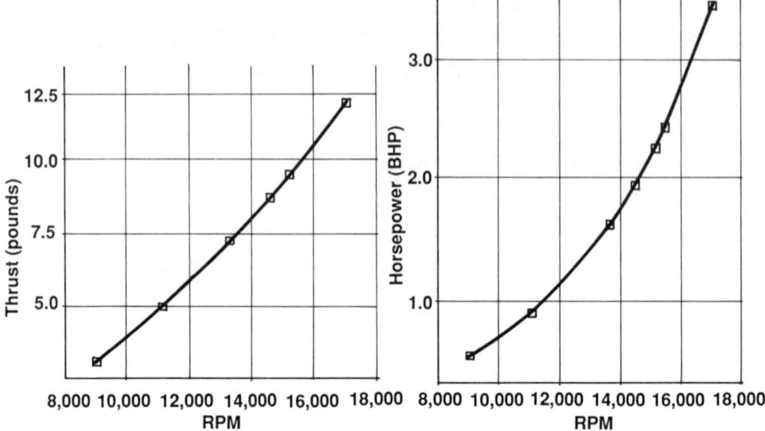

Fig. 3.7. Performance curves for the GLEICHAUF fan.

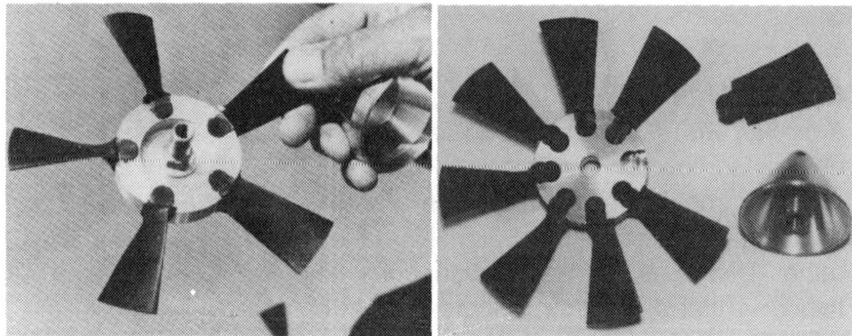

Fig. 3.8. The apparent resemblance between the: (a) HYPERFAN and (b) HURRICANE fan blades, and root fixing arrangement.

writing, it seems that the range of HURRICANE fans offered by Mr. Korney will provide a modeller with a choice of (a) impeller diameter (b) number of blades (c) blade pitch, and (d) a tractor or pusher configuration. The concept is similar to the HYPERFANS marketed by Rossi several years ago. Fig. 3.8 illustrates the resemblance. The HYPERFAN was designed by Aldo Cantelli and manufactured by Piero Caiono of Asti, near Turin in Italy. The impeller was produced using a high quality carbon fibre reinforced injection moulded blade having a cylindrical styled root that mirrored full size turbine practice. The blade root fitted a cylindrical slot milled partway through an aluminium alloy hub and was retained by an aluminium spinner. The HYPERFAN impellers were offered in three sizes as replacements for BYROJET, TURBAX, and AXIFLO 40 impellers.

No shroud unit assembly or engine mount was offered with the

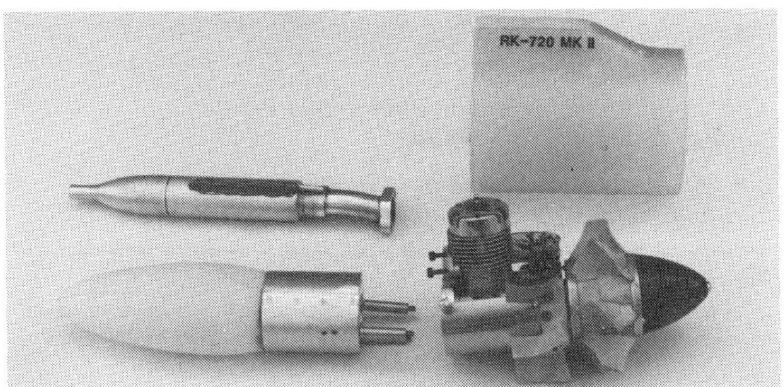

Fig. 3.9. RK 720 MkII fan unit.

HYPERFAN impeller and, in that sense, it differs from the HUR-RICANE fan. The HURRICANE fan also features a spinner that can be used either with a belt or cone-type starter.

The quality of the components appears to be good and the idea of a specially tailored fan is attractive to those modellers wishing to experiment with different engines, or facing particular installation problems. It should be borne in mind, however, that very different stator assemblies would be required for, say, 8-bladed and 5-bladed impellers of the same pitch and diameter.

No performance figures are available at the time of writing.

Jet Age Fans

Supplier: Jet Age Model Aircraft Co., Jet Age is another American manufacturer offering a range of fans to suit different engines, although the diameters are restricted to two sizes; nominally 5 and 6 inch. The blade is very unusual, being shaped like a scimitar with a forward curving profile very much like the blades being developed for full size *unducted* fans. Earlier blades manufactured from glass-filled nylon were prone to failure, but the introduction of carbon fibre reinforced material appears to have solved that problem. The manufacturer claims that the impellers are the only true axial drive impellers available at present.

The fans are of the conventional tractor type with the engine mounted on a centrebody supported by a single row of stator blades. The manufacturer advocates a simple vibration absorbing mounting system.

At the time of writing no performance figures are available.

Micromold Fan

Supplier: Chart-Micromold This fan unit, based on the designs of

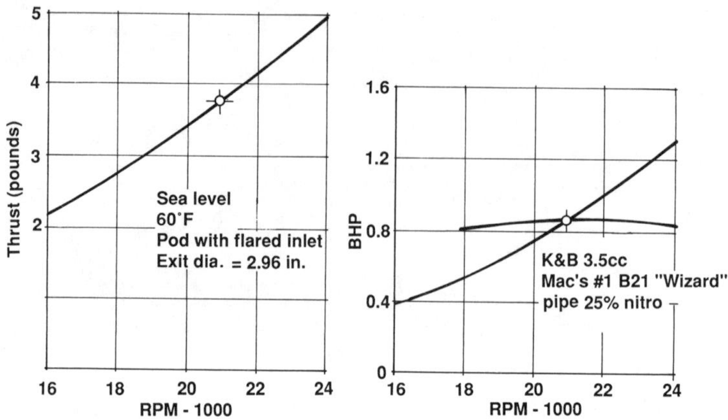

Fig. 3.10. Performance curves for RK720 fans.

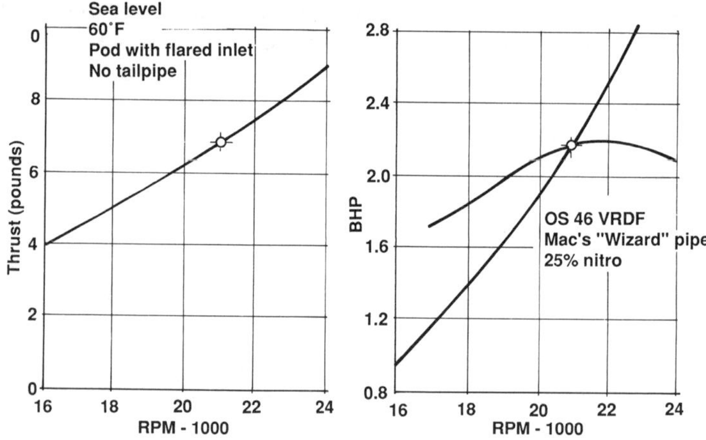

Fig. 3.11. Performance curves for RK740 fans.

P.E. and Marcus Norman, is the least expensive on the market, yet it has an efficient and flexible impeller that has found application with a number of scratch builders and kit manufacturers. In fact, the Micro-mold fan unit is really little more than an impeller/spinner assembly (Fig. 1.11). A simple shroud is provided together with some plywood blanks for stator blades but the modeller is expected to provide his own engine mount. Originally designed for use with the Super Tigre X40 and X45 pylon racing engines, the 5-bladed impeller was sufficiently robust. The manufacturer realised that the front and back plastic plates that retained the blades needed further support if much more powerful engines were to be used, and provided a large metal disc for that purpose. If more blades are to be used with even larger engines, however, carefully machined front and rear locking discs are required. Such discs, together with fully assembled impellers, can be obtained from Turbofan and the Thorpe Brothers.

These impellers, if turned down to the appropriate diameter, may be substituted for the standard impeller in a TURBAX I fan. This gives a slight improvement in static thrust. Belt or cone starting can be used.

RK-740 (MkIII) and RK-720 (MkII) Fans
Supplier Kress Jets Inc. Although Bob Kress no longer markets the AXIFLO fan units for which he is so well known (the RK-049, RK-20B and RK-40), he is still very much involved in design and manufacturing the RK-740 which is similar in external dimensions to the RK-20B but can accept twice the engine capacity. He has also followed this line with the RK-720 (Figs. 3.9 & 3.10), which fits a .20 engine into a fan of similar dimensions to the old RK-049. This has been achieved, in part, by increasing the number of blades from 5 to 7 although the same basic layout is maintained. An unusual feature of the fans is the extension tube that brings the carburettor outside the fan shroud.

Bob Kress claims 7 pounds thrust for the RK-740 using a K&B 7.5 engine at 21,000 rpm (Fig. 3.11). This should allow very high thrust-to-weight ratios to be achieved in small models originally designed with the RK-20B in mind.

Both units are tractor types suitable for use with normal cone starters. A considerable amount of assembly is required. Bob intends to introduce a new fan, the RK-709, designed for use with the Cox TD09 or Enya 11CX Engines. Blade tip diameter is only 3.1 inches with an expected thrust level around 2 pounds, depending on the engine.

Thorjet Fan
Supplier: Thorjet The Thorpe Brothers (Peter and Paul) have led the way in ducted fan technology for many years in the UK. Their prolific designs of scale model jets are all based on the .45 fan/engine combination, so it was natural that they should wish to develop their own fan. The THORJET is based on the Micromold impeller but with an original design of shroud, stator and centrebody. The fan is of the normal tractor configuration and comes virtually ready to bolt onto rails in the aircraft or test stand (Fig. 3.12). It is a particularly robust unit that has found wide acceptance in England and farther afield. It comes supplied with an engine cover cap and is provided with very

Fig. 3.12. A THORJET, installed in an F104 Starfighter.

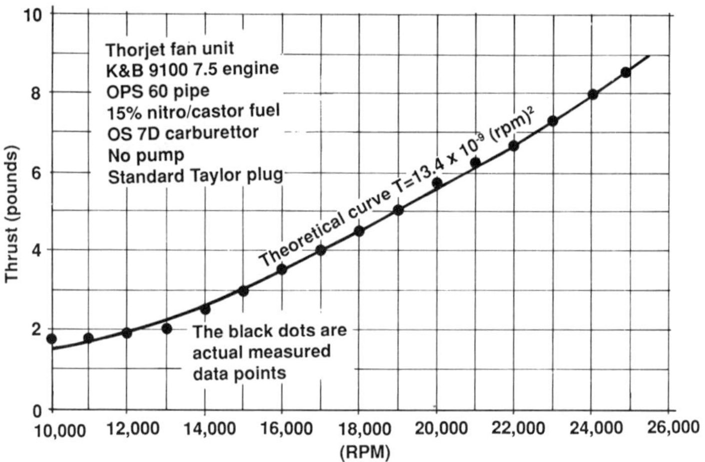

Fig. 3.13. Thrust versus rpm curve for the THORJET fan unit, measured on a thrust stand without an inlet or outlet duct. The theoretical curve seems to be almost straight due to the displaced rpm axis, see Chapter 2. (*courtesy Ron Sweeney*)

detailed instructions and guidance for its operation. The fan is suited to the K&B .45 (front and rear rotor), OPS 45, Picco 45, and OS46 engines.

Fig. 3.13 shows that the fan unit produces over 8 pounds of thrust at 24,700 rpm without the advantage of a properly designed inlet and

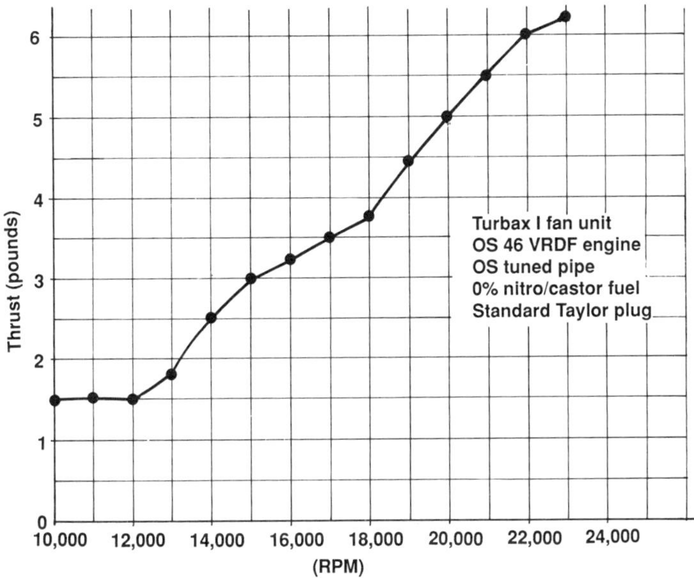

Fig. 3.14. Thrust versus rpm curve for TURBAX I unit (*courtesy Ron Sweeney*)

outlet system. It is likely, therefore, that a similar thrust could be achieved by this unit when carefully installed in a model. The fan is suited to both belt and cone starting. The THORJET has recently been offered in forms utilising up to nine rotor blades so that it can be tailored to suit larger, more powerful engines.

Turbax Fans
Supplier: Jet Hangar Hobbies The origins of the TURBAX fan unit were described in Chapter 1 (Fig. 1.6). The fan is shown in cross section in Fig. 2.2. Both the TURBAX I and III units derive from the original SCOZZI fan, the main differences in the TURBAX III being a wider centrebody mount to take a larger engine (up to .80 cubic inch) and a specially reinforced spinner. Both units are tractor types with a single row of stator blades supporting the centrebody. Apart from the aluminium alloy centrebody and brackets for rail mounting, the remaining components are injection moulded glass fibre reinforced nylon. There is relatively little assembly work to do other than fitting the stators. Starting is by either the cone or belt method.

Thrust versus rpm data are given in Fig 3.14 for a TURBAX I unit mounted in a thrust stand. No inlet was fitted so there is little doubt that the thrust of 6.2 pounds at 22,600 rpm could be improved considerably by a bellmouth intake. Nevertheless, the results are probably a fair indication of what to expect in a model. The fan is well suited to the K&B 7.5 and OS.46 DF engines.

No comparable thrust figures are available for the TURBAX III. As the impeller geometry is identical for both fans, a more powerful engine will obviously turn it at higher rpm, and hence produce more thrust. The manufacturer, Larry Wolfe, claims that it is suited to aircraft weighing up to 15 pounds.

Viojett Fan

Supplier: Bob Violett Models This fan represents the most advanced engineering design available today (Fig. 1.15). The relatively small 4.6 diameter impeller will absorb 4 horsepower and generate over 11 pounds of thrust when fitted with a suitable inlet and mounted on a test stand. The high efficiency claimed for the unit is due to the sophisticated computer-aided design work of Lee Anderson, a professional engineer in an aerospace firm. The area ruling concept has already been explained in Chapter 2, Fig. 2.5. Apart from the shroud shape and fairings, there are several other unusual features in this otherwise conventionally configured tractor fan. A large 'beak-shaped' stator integral with the aluminium alloy centrebody diverts the airflow around the engine cylinder casting, but a slot in the stator allows some air to be directed around the cylinder head for cooling purposes. A remote needle valve is attached to the top front of the shroud to facilitate convenient carburettor adjustment, and shock absorbing rubber mounts allow the fan to be bolted to a mounting rail attached to the fuselage. It is claimed that reduced vibration levels lead to reduced blade tip wear and, hence, greater efficiency. Starting is normally carried out by means of a starter extension which engages a socket head cap screw in the centre of the spinner.

Most of the assembly work is done by the manufacturer, including balancing the impeller. All plastic parts are carbon fibre filled to provide greater strength and rigidity.

The fan is designed primarily for use in conjunction with the KBV.72 and .80 engines which were developed especially for this application and turn the fan at about 22,000 rpm. The manufacturer will also pre-drill the engine mounts to suit the OS77DF or Rossi 65 engines, if required.

This completes the description of all commercial fan units believed to be available at the time of writing. It is not intended to be used as a

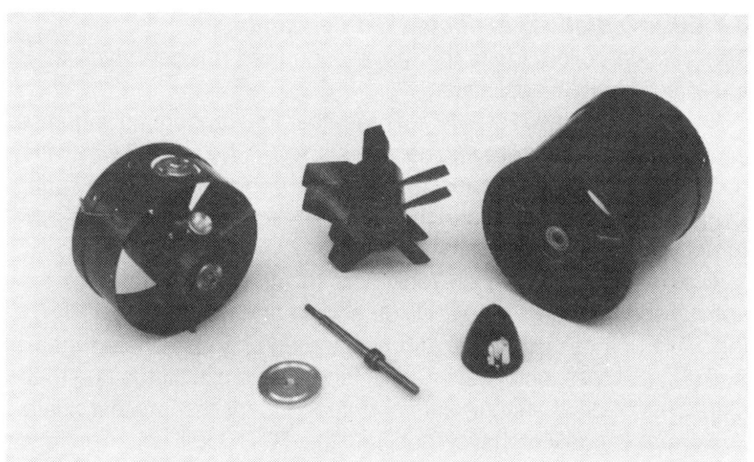

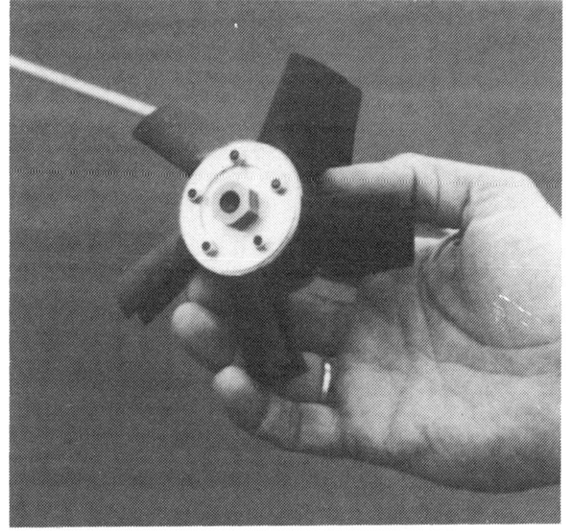

Fig. 3.15.
Experimental fans with 'double' impellers. (a) RK209 (note shaft extension and front rotor bearing). (b) MICROMOLD (note blades are 'in-line').

buyers' guide. The prospective purchaser is advised to seek further information from the suppliers and from those modellers he knows who have used the units. Above all, beware of claimed thrust figures. Most reputable manufacturers are wary of quoting any data knowing that the measured values are so dependent on the way the fan is installed in the model or test stand, not to mention the fuel, plug, pipe etc. that are used. In any case, the only value that can be measured (without the use of a wind tunnel) is static thrust, whereas dynamic thrust is of paramount importance once the model is in the air. The thrust figures I have mentioned should only be used as a very rough guide as to whether the fan might be suited to a particular application.

3.4 Other initiatives in ducted fan development

This section covers ideas that have been tried out but have not yet found commercial application.

Bob Kress put two RK-049 fans together in a tandem arrangement (in line astern). The front engine was started in the normal way with a cone starter on the spinner, but the rear engine required a spring-loaded bevel gear to engage the shaft. The mechanical arrangement turned out to be quite impractical but thrust increased by 59%.

The next approach Bob took was to attach two impellers to a special shaft connected to a TD-09 engine and run this in an RK 049 fan. This unit ran quite well and was temporarily designated the RK 209 (Fig. 3.15(a)), but it never achieved commercial status due to the extra cost of drive attachments and supports for the impeller shaft.

Several modellers have modified the BYROJET impeller in an attempt to increase performance. Bob Thacker's successful blade tapering experiment has already been mentioned (Fig. 2.7). Ralph Saldivar sliced the impeller in a plane perpendicular to the axis of rotation thus producing two, nearly identical, but thinner impellers. The blades were reprofiled and the impellers refitted to the engine, but with the blades offset to various extents to give a range of solidities. Some thrust improvements were noted but not enough to justify the effort.

Other attempts have been made to attach two BYROJET impellers onto a single engine with an extended crankshaft. No results are available but there is clearly a grave risk of fatiguing the crankshaft unless an additional front support is provided. Ian Cooke carried out extensive flight tests with two Micromold impellers turned down slightly in diameter and fitted to a Rossi 65 engine in a TURBAX III fan (Fig. 3.15[b]). The tests were very successful, in that thrust and flight performance improved markedly without the need to run the engine at the very high speeds experienced with the normal TURBAX III impeller. Unfortunately, crankshaft fatigue failures eventually forced him to abandon the experiments but not before he found that the greatest improvement was achieved with the blades on the second impeller directly behind the blades on the front impeller (Fig. 3.15[b]). This arrangement gave minimum solidity but, reasoned Ian, the 'slot' effect so produced might have improved the lift coefficient of the blade pair.

4 THE ENGINE

The ducted fan engine is a special machine, differing from the general sports engines with which most modellers are familiar, in that it must produce its peak power at much higher rpm. Not only that, but the power must be as high as possible commensurate with easy starting and throttling characteristics. These general requirements are shared with marine and pylon racing engines which have provided the base from which the ducted fan engine has been developed. As mentioned in Chapter 3, only one manufacturer (Bauer of West Germany) has designed a fan specifically to suit a normal sports engine, but even that fan is more commonly used with the currently available special ducted fan engines.

For the purposes of this book, all further discussion will be confined to engines that have been specially designated as ducted fan engines by their manufacturers, although this is not intended to exclude consideration of any other high performance engines. As all ducted fan engines are intended to be used with tuned pipes, this chapter also deals with the selection and operation of the pipe. Finally a short section on the glow plug concludes this treatment of the 'engine room'.

4.1 Choice of engine

Table 4.1 lists all designated ducted fan engines believed to be available at the time of writing.

Certain features are common to most ducted fan engines. These are mentioned here rather than in the descriptions of individual engines that follow.

a) All the above engines have ringless pistons.

b) All utilize the following materials combinations:

aluminium piston in a chromium plated brass liner (ABC)

TABLE 4.1 LIST OF SPECIAL DUCTED FAN ENGINES TOGETHER
WITH MANUFACTURERS PERFORMANCE DATA

Manufacturer	Engine Capacity (cubic inches)	Weight (grams)	Horsepower (bhp)	Speed rpm	Fuel
K and B	.45	374	2.3	23,500	
KBV	.72	623	4.0	23,000	
OPS	.21	240	1.5	28,500	0% Nitro
OPS	.40	340	2.2	26,500	0% Nitro
OPS	.45	360	2.3	25,000	0% Nitro
OPS	.60	550	3.5	22,000	0% Nitro
OPS	.67	550	4.2	22,500	50% Nitro
OPS	.80	630	4.5	21,000	50% Nitro
OS	.25	227	1.1	22,000	
OS	.46	379	1.9	23,000	
OS	.77	630	3.9	22,000	
PICCO	.40	600	2.2	26,500	
PICCO	.45	600	2.3	26,500	
PICCO	.60	840	3.4	22,000	
PICCO	.67	840	3.5	22,000	
PICCO	.80	840	5.5	23,000	
ROSSI	.90	990	5.9	22,000	
WEBRA	.80	—	3.1	23,000	

or the equivalent system patented by OS Engines (AAC).

c) All are rear exhaust engines. This arrangement is more convenient than a side exhaust in terms of accommodating the tuned pipe within the duct, and also improves performance slightly.

d) All engines are rear induction apart from the smaller OPS .21, OS25 and K&B 7.5 cc (9100) engines. The main advantage of a rear induction system is improved performance but it is also convenient in that a front induction carburettor can interfere with the stator blade arrangement, or even the impeller, unless a crankshaft extension is used. A long crankshaft overhang is, of course, undesirable from the point of view of vibration and crankshaft fatigue.

e) All the engines use Schneurle porting or similar. The improved combustion and scavenging conditions this feature introduces make it virtually essential in all modern high power engines.

f) All the engines have relatively high exhaust port timings suited to the use of tuned pipes.

g) Most of the engines have large carburettor bores, high compression ratios and are designed to accept high nitromethane fuels, if desired. All these features are designed to improve performance and will be referred to later.

h) Another common, though less desirable, feature of ducted fan engines is their high cost. This is partly due to the relatively low sales volume but it also results from the need for high quality materials, close tolerances, difficult machining and careful finishing/assembly which is essential if high performance is to be accompanied by high reliability.

K&B engines

Manufactured by K&B Manufacturing The K&B 7.5 (9100 series) was the first and, until the early 1980s, the only specially designated ducted fan engine. Its design was based on the very successful racing engines produced by John Brodbeck, and the early adaptation of the K&B 40S in the SCOZZI fan. The new engine (Fig. 4.1) served as a reasonable introduction to ducted fans for thousands of enthusiasts, especially when it was coupled to the TURBAX I fan.

Apart from the inconvenience of the front induction arrangement, the combination of the Perry pump and carburettor proved difficult to adjust. A special high performance package was introduced which eliminated the pump and used an all-metal K&B carburettor; also the new cylinder liner had an increased exhaust port timing. The cylinder head insert was also changed. This new package worked well if fuels with 15% or more nitromethane were used, but such fuels are less

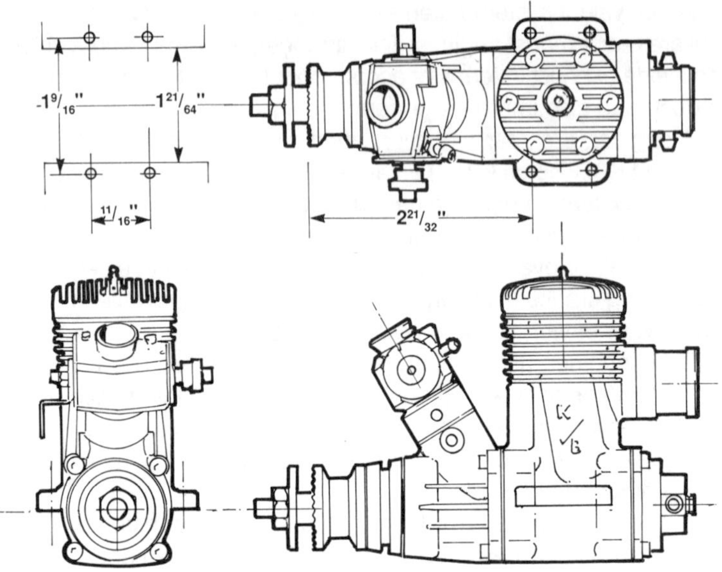

Fig. 4.1. The K&B 7.5cc 9100 series engine was the first to be produced specifically for ducted fan application.

commonly available (and more expensive) in Europe than in the USA.

Very recently, a number of special K&B 45 engines have been delivered to Kress Jets in the USA and Turbofan in the UK. These engines differ from the 9100 Series in that they are rear induction engines. The exhaust ports are especially timed and shaped for ducted fan use, and no pump is required. A metal carburettor is used. The result is an engine with somewhat higher power than its progenitor but which exhibits more reliable operating characteristics (Fig. 4.2).

KBV .72 engine

Manufactured by K&B but distributed exclusively by Bob Violett Models. As its name implies, this engine is the result of a joint development programme between Bob Violett and John Brodbeck Jnr, of K&B. Its performance is optimised to match the VIOJETT ducted fan unit but it could be utilised in a number of other high performance fans.

The engine possesses some unusual features (Fig. 4.3). The front bearing housing is integral with the crankcase rather than bolted to it. Separation distance between front and rear bearings is also longer

Fig. 4.2. The new K&B 45 engine differs from the old 9100 series engine in that it uses rear induction.

Fig. 4.3. The KBV .72 was designed by Bob Violett and John Brodbeck Jr. specifically for the VIOJETT fan unit.

than most engines. Both these features aid smooth, vibration-free running. The carburettor was specially designed for ducted fan use by K&B. It features a remote needle valve for easy access, and a separate mid-range adjustment to improve throttle response. There are no metal-to-metal contacts to wear or seize; this is achieved by

heavily anodizing the carburettor barrel and housing. Despite the large choke area, no pump is required provided the fuel tanks are pressurized by the tuned pipe.

A KBV.80 engine has recently been made available. The prime motivation was to allow for the use of tuned pipes with improved noise reduction capability in the belief that they would lead to a modest loss of performance. The new KBV.80 engine, when coupled to a suitable muffled pipe, should provide approximately the same performance as the unmuffled KBV.72.

OPS engines

Manufactured by OPS This famous Italian manufacturer produces the widest range of ducted fan engines. The OPS 45 has been used very successfully in the THORJET fan unit (Fig. 4.4). It is a sturdy, reliable high performance engine which runs well on standard fuels with little, or no, nitromethane. The OPS-67 has been used in DYNAMAX and TURBAX III fan units.

OS engines

Manufactured by OS Engines Manufacturing Co. Ltd. The largest engine manufacturer in the world was relatively slow to enter the ducted fan market. Generally known more for their quality than the power of their engines, they based the OS-46 DF on their remarkably robust marine engine. This ducted fan engine is ideally suited to the TURBAX I, RK-740 and THORJET fan units. Its only weakness

Fig. 4.5. The OS range of ducted fan engines includes the .65VR-DF, .46VR-DF and .25VF-DF sizes. The OS-77 VR-DF appears outwardly similar to the .65 unit except that it has a large heat sink head.

seems to be fatigue failure of the throttle stop screw, which then allows the carburettor barrel to be ejected from its housing.

Until recently there has been a temporary shortage of .20 to .25 fan units to which the OS-25DF could be coupled. Nevertheless, it seems well matched to the RK-720 and AEROJET-25 fans.

The OS-77 DF appears to be an original design bearing little resemblance to the OS-65 other than in external dimensions. The main distinguishing feature is its large finned heat sink cylinder head which is reminiscent of the Rossi ducted fan engines. When the Rossi-81 went out of production, Byron Originals recommended the OS-77 exclusively for their BYROJET, noting that it slightly out-performed the Rossi. Since then, however, Byron have tested the new Rossi-90 and are now recommending its use with their fan. Nevertheless, the OS-77DF remains a very powerful, reliable engine and matches ideally the DYNAMAX, BOSS PRO and BAUER fan units. It can also be fitted to the VIOJETT and TURBAX III fans. All the OS engines run well on standard fuels.

The OS7D carburettor has found favour amongst K&B 7.5 users where it improves performance considerably compared to the Perry carburettor.

All three OS ducted fan engines are shown in Fig. 4.5.

It is rumoured, at the time of writing, that an OS 90 DF engine will shortly be available.

Fig. 4.6. The range of PICCO ducted fan engines now includes a .90 capacity version.

Picco engines

Manufactured by Picco Motors Picco have recently offered a wide range of special ducted fan engines. Reasonable prices are beginning to encourage their application in many fan units. In particular, the Picco 40 and 45 engines match the TURBAX I and THORJET units very well, and the Picco 80 has run well in the BOSS

Fig. 4.7. The R-90 engine is the largest ROSSI has produced for ducted fan application.

PRO and BYROJET fans. The engines seem rugged, if a little on the heavy side, but their excellent pylon and marine racing pedigree should ensure long life (Fig. 4.6).

Rossi engines
Manufactured by Rossi Electronics Bresciana s.r.l. Yet another famous Italian racing name, Rossi was the next manufacturer (after K&B) to produce a special ducted fan engine. It was designed with the BYROJET in mind following discussions with Byron Godberson. The first engine to appear was the .65, shortly followed by the .81. Within a very short time, they became virtually synonymous with the larger fan units such as the BYROJET, BOSS 602, BAUER, GLEICHAUF, TURBAX III and DYNAMAX fans. The Rossi 81 has also been converted to a diesel and used to drive the GLEICHAUF fan. At present, however, the only Rossi ducted fan engine currently being manufactured is the Rossi-90 (Fig. 4.7). Like its predecessors, it utilizes a large heat-sink cylinder head and a rear drum rotor rather than the disc rotor valve favoured by other manufacturers. The carburettor also comes fitted with an in-flight mixture control valve. When connected to a servo this feature not only allows fuel mixture adjustments to be made while the aircraft is flying, thus minimizing the chance of an expensive 'lean run', but also enables safe adjustment of the engine on the ground.

The Rossi-90 is a particularly sturdy engine weighing just under one kilogram (2.2 pounds). It runs well on straight (zero nitromethane) fuel.

Fig. 4.8. An air filter is a 'must', especially for all engines with carburettors that face into the air stream. This filter was produced by ROSSI for their engines when fitted to BYROJET fans.

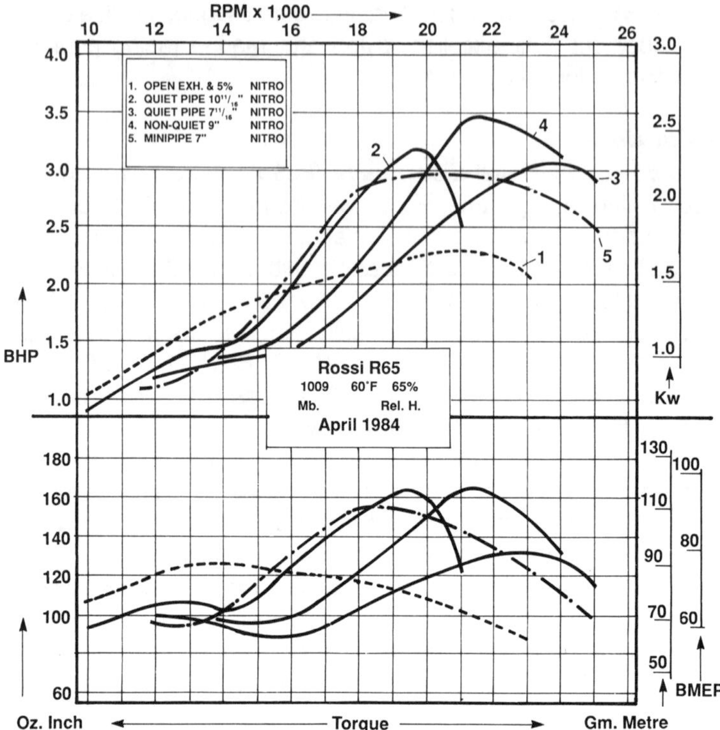

Fig. 4.9. Mike Billinton's engine test data for the ROSSI-65 showing how the tuned pipe arrangement can be used to change the power vs. rpm curve.

Knowing that many of their engines would be used in BYROJET where the carburettor venturi faces into the air stream, Rossi thoughtfully provide a simple air filter (Fig. 4.8), that prevents ingestion of any debris without significantly impairing the performance of stock engines. Very recently, however, we have discovered that the R-81 engine, when specially tuned to provide increased power, benefits from removal of the air filter. This is because the modifications, which are designed to improve breathing capacity, are partially negated by the choking effect of the filter.

Webra engines
Manufactured by Webra Modellmotoren, The Webra Speed 80 fan is a very recent addition to the range of special ducted fan motors. It is based on the .75 engine, features a drum rotor like the Rossi-90, and

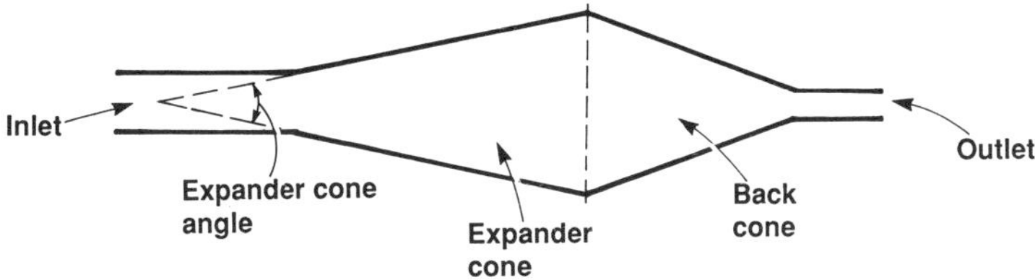

Fig. 4.10. Parts of the tuned pipe.

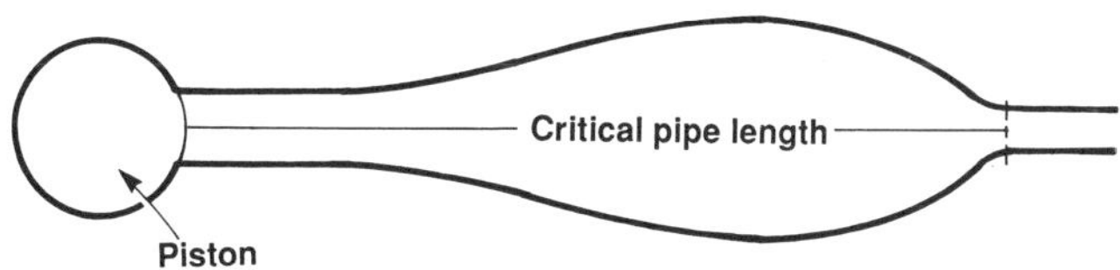

Fig. 4.11. Improved pipe shape (reduces 'peakiness') showing critical pipe length.

delivers 3.1 BHP at 23,000 rpm according to the manufacturer.

4.2 Tuned pipes

As stated earlier all ducted fan engines are designed for use with tuned pipes. Selection of the tuned pipe should be based on the instructions accompanying the engine. The usual preference will be for the engine manufacturer to recommend his own pipes. There are exceptions, however, in that the OS engines seldom seem to be used with OS pipes, and K&B actually recommend MACS pipes for some of their engines.

The prime function of a tuned pipe is to increase the power of the engine. If combined with a suitable expansion chamber, considerable muffling (noise reduction) can be achieved. Another, secondary, function of the pipe is to allow some adjustment of the power versus rpm curve, as mentioned in Chapter 2. Fig. 4.9 shows what can be achieved with the Rossi 65, for example. Finally, the pipe can be used to provide a source of pressure to assist the supply of fuel from the tank to the carburettor. The pressure available from the pipe depends on many factors. Typically, we can expect about 1 psi but this could vary from ½ to 1½ psi depending upon where the pressure nipple is placed along the pipe. The highest pressures are usually associated with the location of the maximum internal diameter of the pipe.

Let us now consider each of these functions in turn:

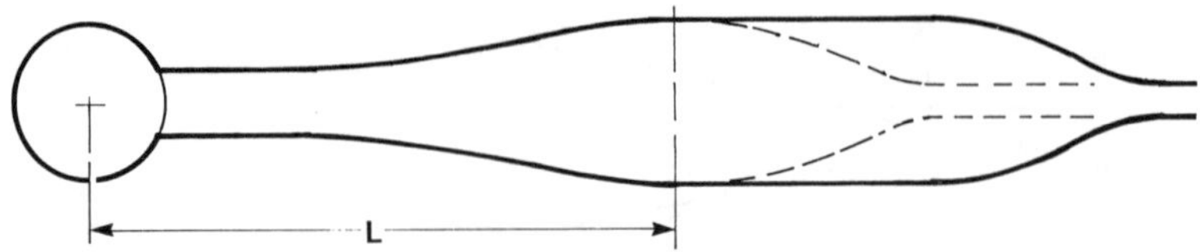

Fig. 4.12. Critical length for setting up a typical commercial tuned pipe fitted with a muffler (or silencing chamber).

a) The tuned pipe as a power booster There are surprisingly few authoritative texts on this subject and I usually find myself referring back to an article in the October 1978 issue of *Radio Control Models and Electronics,* by Kevin Lindsey, designer of ED Powerpipes. Kevin and Bill Wisniewski (of K&B) were probably the first to apply the principles of the tuned exhaust, developed in East Germany after the war, to model two-stroke engines.

The early pipes were powerful but noisy, almost like megaphones, with a wide angled front extractor cone and no muffler chamber. Power gain is very much in proportion to the angle of the expander cone (Fig. 4.10). Similarly with the back cone; it should be angled sharply inwards for maximum supercharging. If the above principles are taken to extremes a 'peaky' pipe results, giving enormous power over a small range of rpm. This would make progressive speed control by throttling virtually impossible as the pipe would act like an on-off switch. The peakiness can be reduced by smoothing the shape changes from inlet to expander to back cone without losing much power, (Fig. 4.11).

So far so good, but the pipe must be a certain length to resonate effectively and give maximum power gain. The pipe length in Fig. 4.11 is proportional to

$$\frac{\text{Pressure pulse velocity x Exhaust port timing}}{\text{(rpm)}}$$

In other words, pipe length must increase if the exhaust timing increases or if the rpm goes down. The pipe length also depends on pressure pulse velocity which goes up with temperature which, in turn, goes up with percentage of synthetic oil in the fuel, compression ratio, lack of cooling, lean running etc. Increased nitromethane content in the fuel reduces the pulse velocity, consequently requiring reduced pipe lengths.

All these effects are generally quite small and the following simple formula, attributed to Dave Marles, allows the pipe length to be estimated quite easily. Fig. 4.12 shows a typical commercial pipe

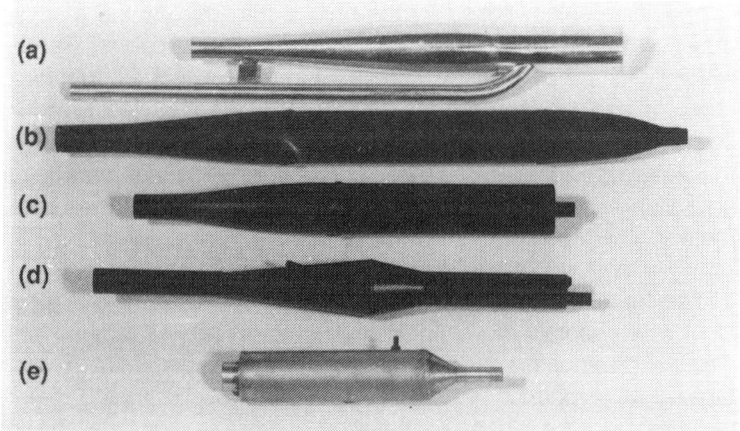

Fig. 4.13. Range of tuned pipes used with ducted fan engines. (a) BYROJET .87/.90 (b) ROSSI .81/.90 (c) ROSSI .60 (d) TURBOFAN .45 (e) IRVINE supersilencer .60

fitted with a muffler. The critical distance, L, is measured from the piston centreline to the end of the expander cone (or maximum pipe diameter location).

$$L \text{ (in centimeters)} = \frac{3660 \times \text{Exhaust timing}}{\text{rpm}} \tag{9}$$

This should give a value of L that is slightly on the long side of the optimum for maximum power gain. This is the right side to err, as it provides for an increase of rpm in the air thus allowing the engine and pipe combination to run closer to its maximum power condition. As an example, consider a K&B 7.5 9100 engine with an exhaust port timing of 172° running in a TURBAX I fan unit at 22,500 rpm. The pipe length would then be

$$L = \frac{3660 \times 172}{22500} = 28 \text{ cm} = 11 \text{ inches}$$

With such a non-critical arrangement it should not make too much difference if the pipe is shortened by a further ½ inch. Although some increase in power can be realised by increasing the exhaust port timing, the enthusiastic reader should be cautioned against exceeding 180° as this will tend to make the pipe setting more critical and, hence, difficult to optimize. The pipe length and expander cone angle control the pipe diameter. As was noted earlier a large angle is required for maximum power gain. This increases the diameter, which has an unfortunate side effect for a ducted fan in that it obstructs the flow of air through the duct, hence a compromise is called for, of which Fig. 4.13 (d) is a good example.

Another problem posed by the pipe is the difficulty the modeller may have in containing its length within the duct of a scale jet. Podded installations are particularly vulnerable in this respect. Fortunately a range of 'mini-pipes' has been developed over recent years, typified by the Irvine Supersilencer (Fig. 4.13 [e]). Such pipes are roughly half the length of the normal pipe, but generally do not provide an equivalent power gain and also tend to be a little noisier than a fully muffled tuned pipe.

b) The tuned pipe as a silencer Fig. 4.13 shows a range of pipes, all of which contain a cylindrical section which acts as a muffler into which exhaust gases expand from the resonating portion of the pipe, thus allowing part of their kinetic energy to be dissipated, before escaping from the pipe outlet. Fig. 4.12 shows a section through such a pipe. The effectiveness of the muffling chamber depends on its volume and the material from which it is made. The volume, or size, of the chamber poses obvious problems when placed within a duct.

As far as material is concerned, most pipes are made from aluminium alloy. Unfortunately, this is not ideal for sound absorption, as aluminium is a low density metal and possesses a low damping capacity (it rings like a bell). Recent experiments with steel pipes are showing great promise. Stainless steel is used for the resonating portion, but the muffler chamber is from ferritic steel which is a high damping material. Although steel is more dense than aluminium alloys, it is stronger and allows thinner gauges to be used. It can also be brazed and silver soldered very easily.

The pipe outlet diameter is quite important. If too large, the noise level increases; if too small, the pipe is choked and may cease to function properly. A heavy buildup of carbon in the pipe has the same effect. A large pipe outlet diameter also reduces the effectiveness of the pipe as a fuel tank pressuriser (see next section).

c) The tuned pipe as a fuel pump The pipe doesn't really act as a pump, of course, but it can be used to pressurise the fuel tank. Pipe pressure is usually sufficient to force fuel up a height of at least 12 inches without the assistance of any suction from the carburettor. In most cases, that height would be doubled or even tripled thus avoiding the need to fit a fuel pump for almost all ducted fan installations. Pumps are, in any case, just one more thing to go wrong. Furthermore, some pumps that depend on crankcase pressure fluctuations simply will not function properly at very high rpm, although they may be quite satisfactory for the sports engine at

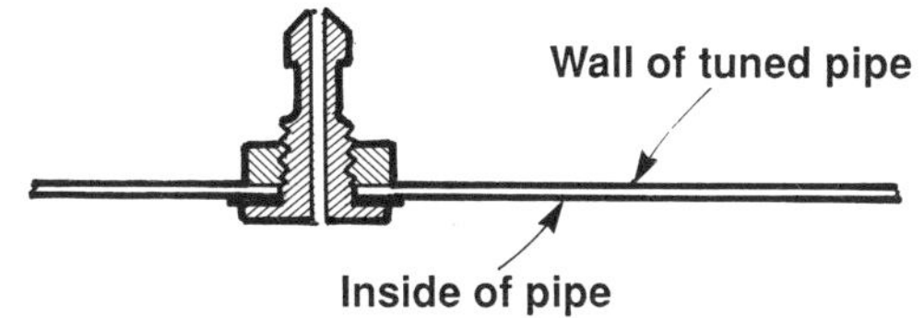

Fig. 4.14. Preferred OPS type of nipple for attaching fuel tank pressure tube to tuned pipe.

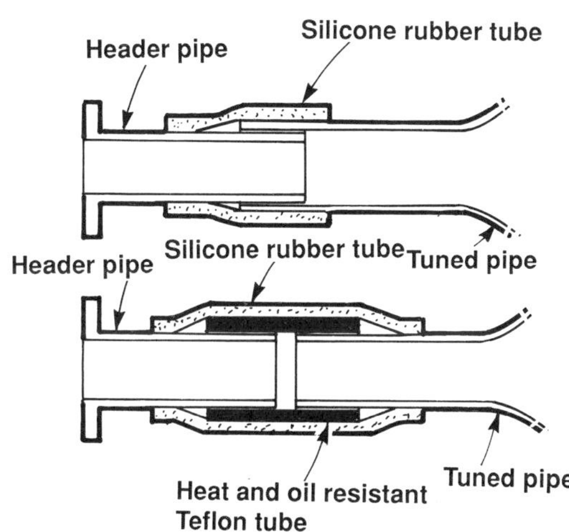

Fig. 4.15. Two methods for connecting the tuned pipe to the header pipe. The Teflon tube should be a tight push fit onto both pipes. The silicone rubber tube should be secured with cable ties at each end.

16,000 rpm.

Although pressurization of fuel tanks by a tuned pipe is easily achieved, it can still cause problems. If pipe pressure is suddenly lost, fuel supply to the engine will be restricted and a lean run or worse (an engine failure) can result. This should not spell disaster for a model boat; similarly, a pylon racer or aerobatic aircraft will usually stand a much better chance of surviving than a heavily loaded scale jet on take-off. In a recent analysis of 300 ducted fan flights, I found that 14% of all 'incidents' (either crashes or aborted flying sessions) were due to failures in the tuned pipe system. The rules for avoiding such incidents are simple.

1) Use thick-walled silicone rubber tube between the tuned pipe nipple and the fuel tank, and protect it from chafing where it passes through the duct wall.

2) Make sure the nipple is secure. I prefer the sort with a shoulder that

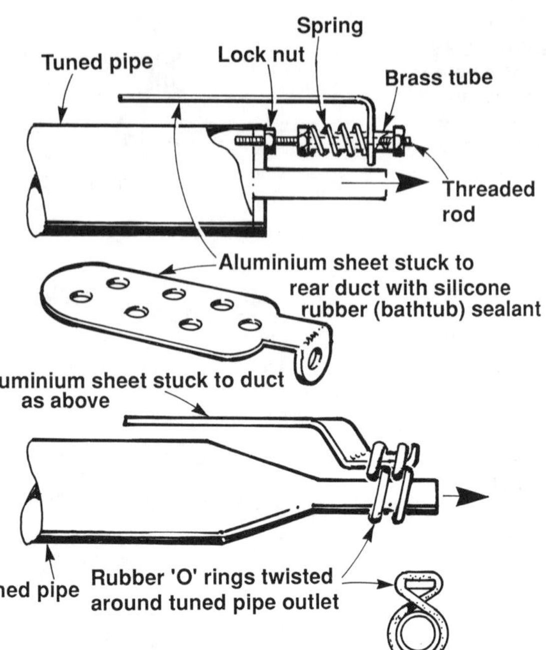

Fig. 4.16. Two methods for providing a flexible rear support for the tuned pipe.

goes inside the pipe, like the OPS nipples (Fig. 4.14). When tightened down, coat the threads with epoxy. Better still, weld or silver solder the nipple in place. This is a simple matter with a steel pipe.

3) The pressure in the pipe corresponds to an axial load of 5 pounds or more, so the pipe must be supported adequately, but flexibly (to allow for expansion and vibration), at both ends. Fig 4.15 shows how to support the pipe at the inlet end, depending upon whether the pipe allows a sliding fit (preferred) or a 'butt' joint. In both cases, the silicone rubber tube *must* be clamped to the pipe with cable ties or metal jubilee clips. If a Teflon (or RTFE) connector is not available (second method), wrap a thin aluminium sheet around the joint — litho plate works well — before slipping the silicone rubber tube into place. Teflon is best because it avoids metal-to-metal contact and hence the possibility of fretting debris passing up the pipe and into the engine. The main purpose of the Teflon however, is to prevent the hot exhaust gases contacting the silicone rubber and causing its deterioration.

Fig 4.16 shows how the opposite end of the pipe can be supported. The same forces that are trying to tear the pipe from the engine are also acting on the header pipe. Sometimes this is bolted to the

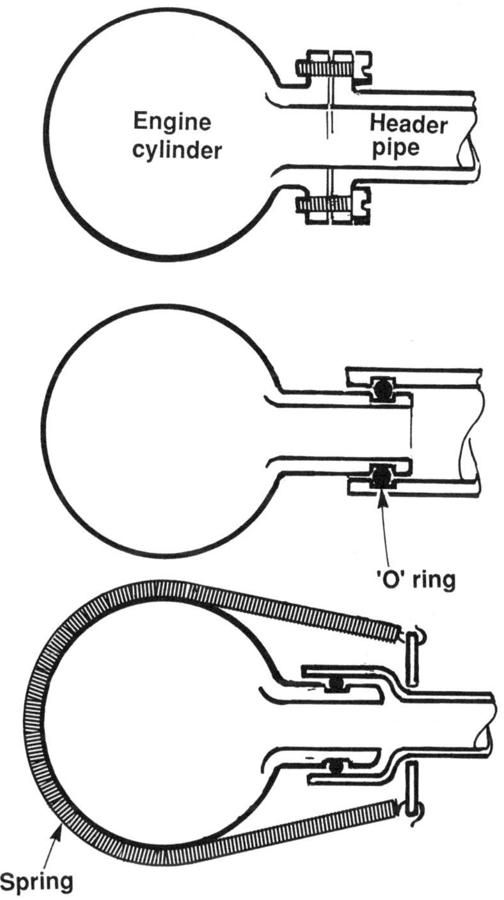

crankcase, in other cases an 'O' ring seal is used, yet another is the 'spigot' arrangement retained by a spring looped round the crankcase. Fig 4.17 shows all three systems.

4.3 The glow plug

Sometimes an engine comes with a plug, sometimes it does not. The first thing is to find out whether a long or short reach plug is required. The engine instructions should tell you. If not, you may have to experiment. Err on the side of caution at first by using a short reach plug or a long reach plug with two or more washers to ensure that it does not contact the piston. Incidentally, the use of an extra plug washer is quite a simple way of lowering the compression ratio slightly.

Plugs do not usually last long in ducted fan engines. Ten flights is usually regarded as excellent. Cold plugs with very thick elements usually last longest, although the thicker platinum-rhodium element makes them more expensive. They can draw more than 5 amps so make sure your power supply can cope. The Rossi R-8 and OPS 300 are good examples of this type of plug. A few engines, particularly those that prefer to run with higher nitromethane fuels, seem to throttle best with a standard, inexpensive glow plug with a thin element that is able to sustain combustion more effectively than a cold plug. The important thing is to find out what suits your engine best and stick to it.

Remember that a plug element can fracture, but will still provide a source of ignition to keep the engine running if the element doesn't disintegrate completely. Elements that break up like that are bad news anyway as they can damage the piston and liner.

Plugs fail for two main reasons (or a combination of both): they either fatigue due to vibration, or creep and distort due to overheating. The cure for the vibration problem is obvious — either eliminate the source of vibration or use a thicker (stronger) element. If the cause is overheating, a thicker element will help. Other ways to minimize overheating are: a) improve cylinder head cooling, b) reduce the compression ratio, c) reduce the nitromethane content, d) improve the lubricant, or e) lengthen the tuned pipe.

5 THE AIRFRAME

5.1 Preliminary considerations

This chapter covers those items over which there is little control if building from kits or plans. With the belief, however, that the reader may one day wish to design his own ducted fan aircraft, or at least modify or customize someone else's design, I will now discuss the fuselage, wing and empennage design, and review appropriate finishing techniques. As in previous chapters, I will concentrate on those issues that are of particular importance to ducted fan aircraft, leaving the reader to consult standard aeromodelling texts where more general information is required.

Firstly a few questions must be answered:

1) Is a scale or sport aircraft required?

2) If scale, what prototype is to be modelled and how far can compromises be made, especially regarding outline?

3) If sport, what characteristics are required?

e.g. docile handling, wide speed envelope, aerobatic capability.

4) What size aircraft (span and length)?

5) How heavy can it be?

6) How much should it cost?

Answers to the above questions will constitute a broad outline specification for the airframe and allow us to make a few important decisions, starting with the choice of engine/fan combination. The most important factor is the desired static thrust-to-weight ratio (T/W) of the finished aircraft (usually based on dry weight — i.e. without fuel). The minimum acceptable ratio for any type of aircraft is T/W = 0.5. For a trainer, a little extra margin is required, say T/W = 0.7. whereas, for a high speed, fully aerobatic, aircraft nothing less than T/W = 1.0 will do. Reference back to the thrust figures in Chapter 3 gives an indication of what fans might be suitable. The fan shroud external diameter will place a limit on the minimum size of airframe, but bear in mind that the engine cylinder head will usually extend beyond the shroud and this will have to be accommodated somewhere. The next step is to estimate the weight of fan unit, engine and tuned pipe. Chapters 3 and 4 contain relevant information but the following examples may be helpful:

TURBAX I + OS 46DF + pipe + ducts weigh 2.3 pounds

VIOJETT + KBV .72 + pipe + ducts weigh 3.4 pounds

The fan units have roughly the same dimensions, thus the airframe would have the same minimum size. If the undercarriage, radio, other hardware and finish is estimated to weigh an additional 2.3 pounds, then the remaining weight will be accounted for by the unfinished airframe itself (fuselage, wings, tail empennage). If it is intended to put the VIOJETT in a high speed sport aircraft with T/W = 1.0, then assuming an installed static thrust of 9 pounds would allow 3.3 pounds for the airframe. This should be relatively easy to attain. If the same demand is placed upon the TURBAX I/OS46DF power plant, then an assumed installed thrust of 7 pounds would limit airframe weight to 2.4 pounds — a much more difficult proposition. On the other hand a T/W = 0.7 would allow a total dry weight of 10 pounds and an airframe weight of 5.4 pounds. Finally, if the TURBAX I/OS46 DF were to power a scale aircraft requiring a minimum T/W = 0.5, then, even allowing for an installed thrust deterioration to 6 pounds due, perhaps, to less than ideal intakes, there would be a massive 7.4 pounds available for the airframe and all the detail a scale enthusiast could reasonably wish for.

If the estimates do not work out so favourably, it will be necessary to re-examine the specification with a view to relaxing the requirements or selecting a new project altogether.

Before moving on to more detailed considerations, one further simple calculation is required. Estimate the wing loading by dividing the total dry weight (expressed in ounces) by the *total projected area* of the aircraft — not just the wing (expressed in square feet). For a small, docile, ducted fan trainer, the wing loading should not exceed 25 ounces per square foot, whereas that figure can be doubled to 50 ounces per square foot for a large, high speed, or scale aircraft.

Assuming the wing loading criterion is satisfied, we will now have decided the weight and size of the aircraft to be modelled, and the fan/engine combination that will power it. The next thing to determine is the internal ducting arrangement for the fan, which will in turn decide where the auxiliary systems fit (electrics, hydraulics, pneumatics etc.) The unusual thing about a ducted fan aircraft is that

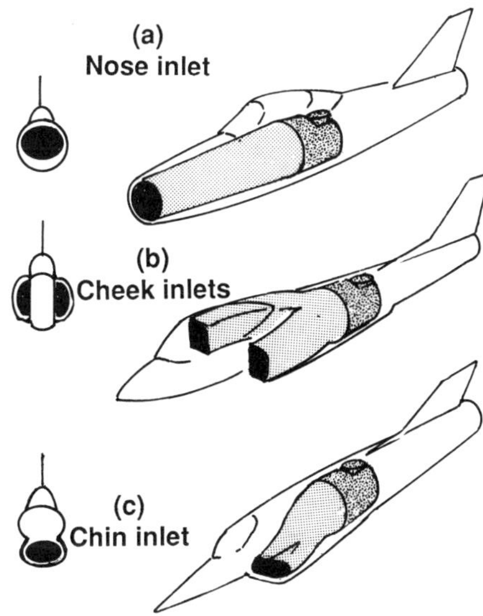

Fig. 5.1. Three basic types of inlet duct arrangement.

the fuselage is really a tube within a tube. Everything apart from the power unit has to fit in between the two tubes. This is quite a demand and some juggling takes place between duct layout and the location of auxiliary equipment (radio, fuel tanks, air tanks etc.) Well, you cannot be an engineer unless you are willing to compromise!

Basically there are only three inlet duct arrangements (Fig. 5.1), of which only the nose inlet (a) poses any particular difficulties. The problem is that there is very little room in front of the fan between the duct and the fuselage for the nose gear retract mechanisms, or to place batteries and servos in order to achieve an acceptable centre of gravity (C.G.) Location of fuel tanks is also difficult. Sometimes there has to be two specially shaped tanks on either side of the duct. Solutions can be worked out, however (Fig. 5.2), even with scale inlets and full ducting to the fan. The solution is much simpler if scale requirements are relaxed sufficiently to allow cheat inlets, in which case the inlet duct could be dispensed with altogether. This is particularly appropriate for a pusher fan installation like the BYRO-JET, where the tuned pipe, engine, and other fitments are forced to clutter the nose inlet area (Fig. 5.3).

There are comparatively few problems with the cheek and chin inlet configurations shown in Fig. 5.1, as the nose area provides ample room for the fuel tank, radio and retract system (Fig. 5.4). This is, no doubt, one reason why so few modern jets (full size or models) feature

Fig. 5.2. The limited space available for equipment installation in nose inlet designs.

Fig. 5.3. How a large auxiliary or 'cheat' inlet simplifies a nose intake installation.

nose inlets.

The next decision is where to put the engine and fan. There is usually a reasonable amount of freedom to manoeuvre, but let us first consider the ideal position from an aerodynamic standpoint. This

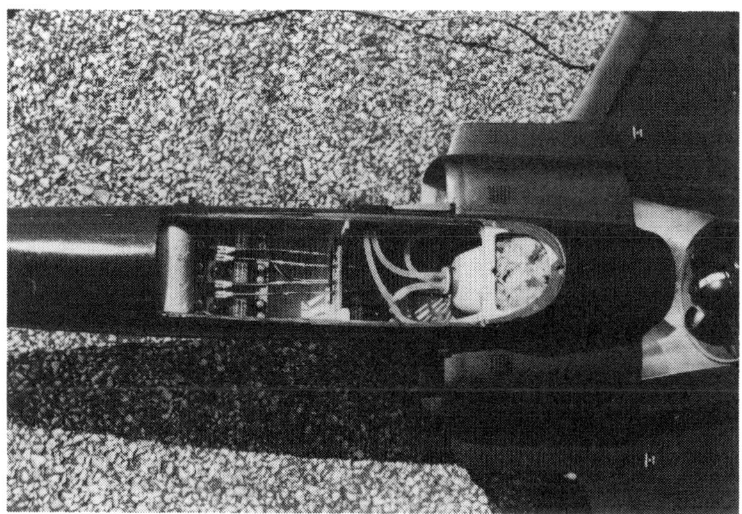

Fig. 5.4. There is spacious accommodation for radio gear and fuel in nose of aircraft with cheek inlets.

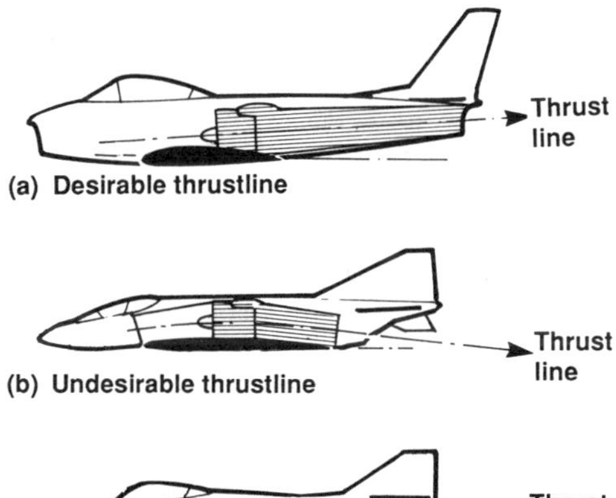

Fig. 5.5. Desirable and undesirable thrustline relationships with respect to wing rigging angle and attitude on ground.

places the fan close to the bottom of the fuselage so that a certain amount of downthrust is possible, (Fig. 5.5 [a]). We are all familiar with the need to get the thrustline correct for propeller driven aircraft; it is just as important for jets except that it is measured in a different place. Two problems can arise if the downthrust is insufficient. The first is that the aircraft may not be able to take off because of the jet reaction forces tending to depress the nose, (Fig. 5.5 [b]). A Swedish friend measured the load on the nose leg of his MiG-25 to be two pounds at zero thrust but it increased to 10 pounds at full thrust. All this extra nose load has to be overcome by downward forces on the tailplane as up-elevator is applied during take-off.

In some cases, the tailplane may not be able to cope. At Abingdon a few years ago, a F-100 Super Sabre made three attempts to take-off. Although the speed appeared more than adequate, the plane refused to rotate and the pilot had to abort. In an act of desperation we 'adjusted' the duct outlet angle in a rather brutal fashion and away it flew at the next attempt. I have seen horizontal vanes placed inside the tailpipe that could be adjusted to act as thrust directors in order to overcome the problem of a bad thrustline. This is very undesirable as it leads to considerable loss of thrust. A somewhat better approach is to fabricate the rear duct so that it inclines upward at the outlet (Fig. 5.5 [c]).

The second consequence of a bad thrustline (as in Fig 5.5 [b]) is that the trim changes dramatically when the engine cuts or is suddenly throttled back. The nose will come up and may require a certain amount of down-elevator for landing! A much worse situation occurs if a take-off is aborted at the last moment; as the throttle is shut the aircraft can leap into the air with a dead engine!

The only other consideration concerning fan location is how far forward it should go in the fuselage. The optimum is close to, or just in front of, the C.G., but so much will depend on the proximity of the inlet(s), wing fixing arrangements, the need to keep the tuned pipe from sticking out of the tailpipe etc.

Centre of gravity (C.G.)

It is impossible to overstress the importance of getting the location of the C.G. right. If it is too far back, the aircraft will be impossible to control. If it is too far forward, it may be impossible to get into the air. If in doubt, try to ensure that, for the first flight at least, the C.G. is a little further forward than it may eventually be located.

There is no shortage of guidance on this subject in other books and magazine articles but, unfortunately, this is almost entirely restricted to propeller-driven aircraft and gliders, for which it is usually quite permissible to ignore the lifting effect of the fuselage when calculating a safe C.G. Unfortunately, this doesn't work too well with jets as they tend to have longer and fatter noses than, say, a glider, Spitfire or Curare. Certain modern jets depend on body lift as much as wing lift — the F104 Starfighter is a good example (Fig. 5.6 [a]). Other exotic lift

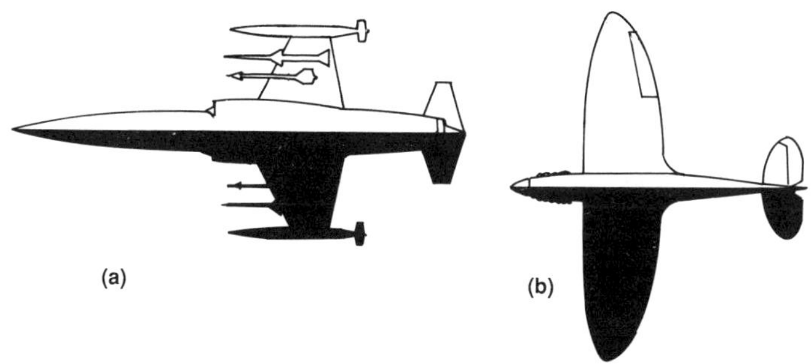

Fig. 5.6. Modern jets such as the F104 Starfighter (a) have much larger body areas relative to wing areas than earlier propeller driven aircraft such as the Spitfire (b). Furthermore, the noses of jets tend to be much longer and therefore destabilize the aircraft.

devices, such as leading edge extensions, complicate the matter still further. This is why, when calculating wing loading, it is necessary to consider the total projected area of the aircraft — body and all.

The effect of a fat body and long nose is to act in opposition to the tailplane or horizontal stabilizer, as it is so aptly called in the USA. In other words, the nose, if large enough, can destabilize the aircraft unless the C.G. is placed well forward. The vital rule is that:

THE C.G. MUST ALWAYS LIE IN FRONT OF THE A.C.

The A.C. is the Aerodynamic Centre of the entire aircraft. The A.C. of the wings can be estimated quite easily (Fig. 5.7). The A.C. of the

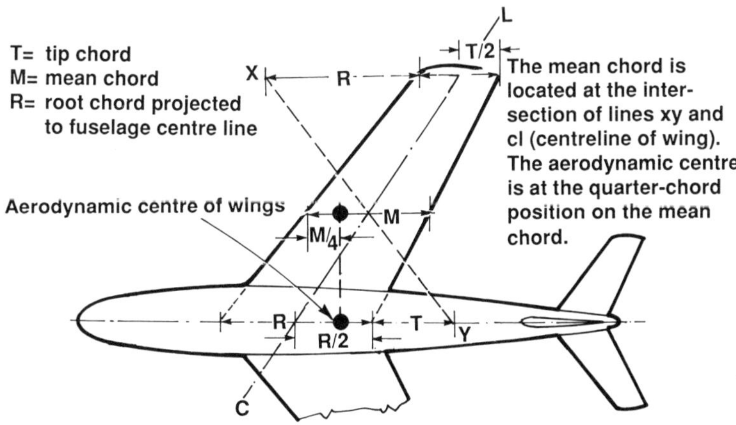

Fig. 5.7. How to find the aerodynamic centre of a swept and tapered wing.

tailplane can be found by an identical method, but it is more difficult to estimate the fuselage A.C. location. Furthermore, the efficiency of the fuselage as a lifting surface is not so great as the wing or tailplane, thus it becomes quite a complicated problem to estimate, with any precision, the location of the A.C. of the whole aircraft. Fortunately there are several ways around the difficulty.

1) For a simple swept, or straight, wing jet of conventional configuration (not a canard) such as the MiG-15, Sabre, BAC Hawk, Hunter etc., try putting the C.G. at roughly 10% of the mean chord (Fig. 5.7) rather than the 25% position which is usually regarded as totally safe for a glider, Spitfire or Curare. It may be possible to move it back a bit after the first flight, but experience has shown that a value between 10 and 15% is about right for the jets mentioned above.

2) A good way to determine the C.G. position for a scale aircraft is to look at the location of the main wheels on the full size version and then place the C.G. of the model 3 or 4 inches in front of this position (assuming tricycle undercarriage). This should put it well in front of the C.G. for the full size, but this is necessary because the model needs to be more stable than the full size version. The pilot of the model lacks the 'seat of the pants' feel of the guy who sits in the cockpit. Added to that, certain modern fighter aircraft are inherently unstable anyway and need a computer to fly them.

3) A third method for estimating the C.G. is to draw onto stiff card a plan view or silhouette of the aircraft to a scale that gives a length around 10 inches. Cut out the silhouette and attach a simple fin for directional stability and gently test-fly it. If it stalls, keep adding weight to the nose (paperclips should do) until a stable glide results. Balance the paper aeroplane on a knife edge to determine the C.G. and transfer this location to your detailed design drawings.

A final word on the C.G: it is one thing to know where it *should* be, but quite another to know where it *actually* is. I strongly advise

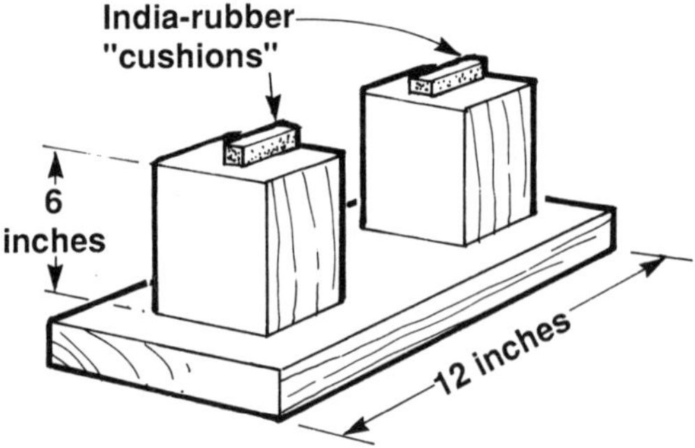

Fig. 5.8. Jig for measuring CG location.

building a simple jig out of scrap timber (Fig. 5.8). The complete aircraft, without fuel, is placed on the jig with its wings resting on the two india-rubber cushions (approximately 1 x ¼ inch). It is then moved backwards or forwards until it just balances. Mark the location of both rubber supports where they contact the wings, and draw a line between the two locations. Where the line crosses the centre line of the fuselage is the actual C.G. Check it against the plan view location shown on your drawing.

5.3 To Cheat or not to cheat? auxiliary air intakes

More has been written about the intake design (both scale and auxiliary intakes or cheater holes) than any other feature of ducted fan airframe design. Bob Kress was probably the first person to apply some science to it. If static thrust was the only concern, the bellmouth inlet (Fig. 2.4) would be perfectly adequate but, unfortunately this type of inlet is very inefficient at high speed, causing the dynamic thrust to suffer. A suitable compromise is shown in Fig. 5.9. The trick is to get a good rounded lip, like the leading edge of an aerofoil section, so that the air can be drawn around the lip and into the fan without separating from the surface. The F-86 Sabre nose inlet is a good example. Small pieces of grass or fluff can be sucked from the sides of the fuselage and drawn into the inlet from as far back as 4 or 5 inches from the nose.

Kress found that, compared with the measured thrust for the bellmouth inlet, there was virtually no detectable reduction for the 'optimised' inlet in Fig 5.9. If the contoured inlets were removed altogether, with no attempt to improve the fan shroud inlet lip, the measured thrust fell to 65% of the bellmouth thrust for the RK-40 fan and to 55% for the Scozzi fan.

So much for the shape of the inlet; but we also need to know how

Fig. 5.9. Optimum inlet shape for static and dynamic thrust.

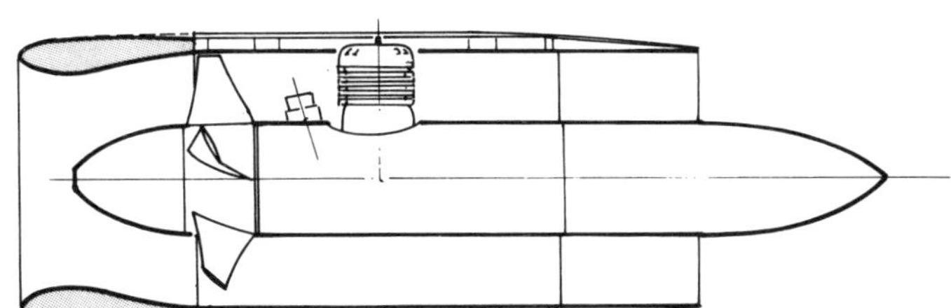

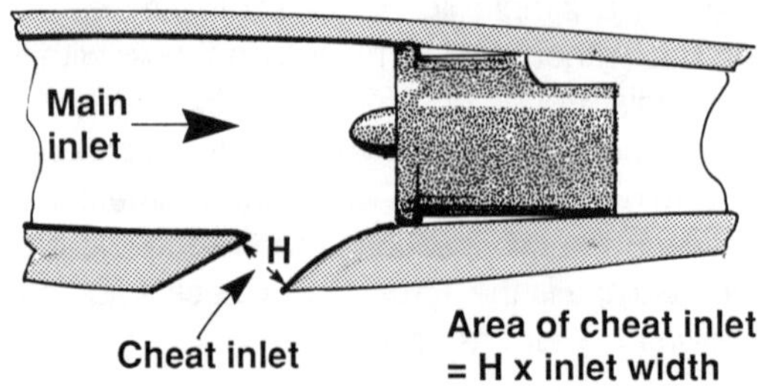

Fig. 5.10. Effective throat area of an auxiliary or cheat intake.

large it should be. Kress continued his experiments and found that an optimised pod inlet could be reduced in area to as little as 40% of the area swept by the fan blades without dropping the thrust below 85% of the bellmouth datum thrust. However, auxiliary inlets cut through the fuselage sides proved to be very inefficient even with rounded lips. The throat area (Fig. 5.10) of these inlets needed to be almost twice as large as the area swept by the fan blades if significant thrust losses were to be avoided.

Although the validity and usefulness of Kress' conclusions have been questioned from time-to-time, it is this author's experience that the Kress guidelines are worth following. Having flown an F-86 Sabre with and without a cheat intake through the wing, I can report that the static thrust fell from 7 pounds to 6 pounds when the cheat inlet was closed. The actual areas are as follows:

Area swept by fan blades	14.6 square inches	
Area of scale nose inlet	6.0 "	"
Area of cheat inlet throat	18.0 "	"
Total area of nose and cheat inlets	24.0 "	"

Although the acceleration of the Sabre was not so good with the cheat inlet blocked, as might be expected with a lower static thrust, the plane could take off in roughly the same distance as before. Furthermore the top speed actually increased. The large hole in the wing (Fig. 5.11) had been doing several things. Firstly, it had increased the drag of the aircraft. This will be true of virtually all cheat intakes. Secondly, it had not just been ineffective at high speed, it had actually dissipated the beneficial 'ram-effect' of the nose inlet. It is quite likely that air was escaping from the cheat inlet at high speed rather than entering through it. Thirdly, at low speeds, particularly during take-off, the hole destroyed some lift by drawing air from under the wing. Thus the aircraft had to travel faster before the lift increased to the point where it would fly. Finally, the cheat inlet produced symptoms similar to a bad thrustline in that the trim would change violently if the engine stopped suddenly. This was because the wing lift was restored as the

Fig. 5.11. The large cheat intake in the wing of Ian Cooke's Sabre.

suction through the cheat inlet dropped.

The conclusion is that cheat inlets are undesirable, provided there is sufficient thrust from the scale inlet(s) to allow take off in a reasonable distance. Some models having to fly off rough grass fields or with marginal thrust capability may still have to cheat a little! How then is this best achieved?

If the cheat inlet *must* be in the wing, put it as far forward as possible and keep its size to a minimum (Fig. 5.12). An even more extreme example is shown in Fig. 5.13, where the two cheat inlets have forward facing louvres.

It is usually impossible to place the cheat inlet somewhere other than through the wing without destroying the appearance of the aircraft, unless some form of blow-in door is used. Fig. 5.14 shows Paul Thorpe's Sabre with blow-in doors that are scarcely visible, just behind the gun panel. In fact the doors are only obvious when the aircraft is taking off; at high speed the ram effect takes over and the doors close again.

The ram effect is quite important to model jet flight and justifies an attempt to understand it. The faster an aeroplane flies, the greater the dynamic pressure (sometimes called velocity pressure) it experiences at any forward facing surfaces. This pressure rise also occurs at forward facing inlets, though not at cheat inlets which are flush with

Fig. 5.12. If a cheat inlet must be made through the wing, keep it small and as far forward as possible.

Fig. 5.13. Small louvred cheat inlets in Ron Sweeney's F-20 Tigershark should have minimal effect on wing lift, but they may not improve the thrust much, either! Note the Leading Edge Root Extensions (LERX).

Fig. 5.14. Paul Thorpe's Sabre has cheat inlets that are hidden by blow-in doors on the fuselage sides, just behind the gun panel.

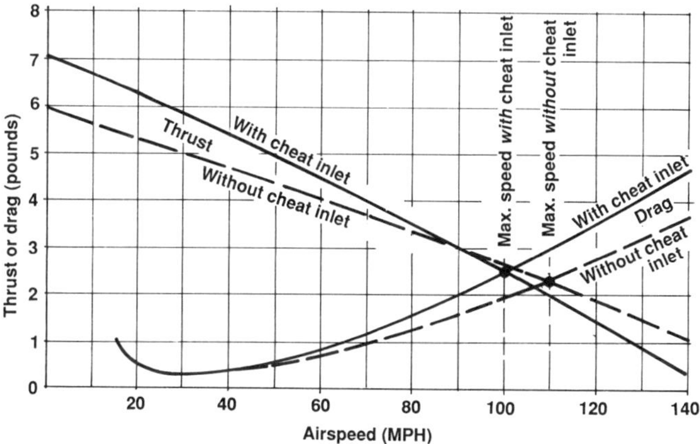

Fig. 5.15. How elimination of a cheat intake can result in an increase in maximum speed.

the sides or bottom of the fuselage. The ram effect augments the pressure in front of the fan, which allows the fan to accelerate the air passing through it more than would otherwise be possible, thereby producing more dynamic thrust and even higher speeds.

Fig. 5.15 shows how the elimination of a cheat intake can make an aircraft fly faster. The solid curves correspond to the drag and dynamic thrust (of an F-86 Sabre with a cheat inlet) plotted against flying speed. The way the curves are derived will be discussed later. For the moment, note that the point where they cross corresponds to the maximum speed attainable in level flight (100 mph) since thrust is exactly equal to drag at that speed. I have assumed that the cheat inlet removes any possibility of ram augmentation. If the cheat inlet is now blocked off, and the inlet ducts smoothed over where the cheat hole was, three things happen. Firstly, the drag decreases (lower broken line) and, secondly, the static thrust decreases, *but* the dynamic thrust (upper broken line) is augmented by the ram effect so that, at very high speed, it actually exceeds the dynamic thrust obtained *with* the cheat intake. Note that the two broken curves cross at 110 mph which is the new maximum flying speed without the cheat inlet.

5.4 Hatches

Hatches are a virtually unavoidable feature, a necessary evil of ducted fans for the simple reason that everything of interest is tucked away inside the fuselage rather than hung out in front. The general rule is to keep the hatches as few, and as small, as possible commensurate with straightforward operation and maintenance work. Sometimes the hatch can take the form of a removable cockpit and canopy, as with some Byron Originals kits. In others, the hatch needs to expose a huge area to enable engine starting and maintenance work to be carried out (Fig. 5.16 [a]). In some cases, occasional access can be obtained through a cheat inlet or with the wing removed, but usually it is necessary to have at least one hatch on top of the aircraft, often reducing the strength of the structure considerably (Fig. 5.16 [b]). Special attention must always be given to reinforcing the area around any hole in the fuselage, as its strength, particularly with fibreglass structures, depends almost entirely on the integrity of the 'skin'.

The other problems with hatches are how to make them unobtrusive and how to keep the hatch in place. Most designers and builders have their own favourite techniques. Philip Avonds uses screws and flush-fits the edges of the hatch in his F-15 (Fig. 5.16 [a]). Ron Sweeney (Fig. 5.16 [b]) uses a built-up balsa structure that maintains the shape of the hatch very well, and butt-joints the edges of the hatch and fuselage. The hatch is retained by commercial style sprung-loaded hatch latches at either end.

Bob Violett tackles the problem of fitting fibreglass hatches (which tend to distort when cut free) by moulding a special flange into the fuselage structure. Small spigots, or pins, in the hatch then slip into holes in the flange (Fig. 5.17 [a]). Two commercial hatch latches are used, both located in the fuselage. Larry Wolfe of Jet Hangar Hobbies favours the technique shown in Fig. 5.17 (b) for fibreglass structures,

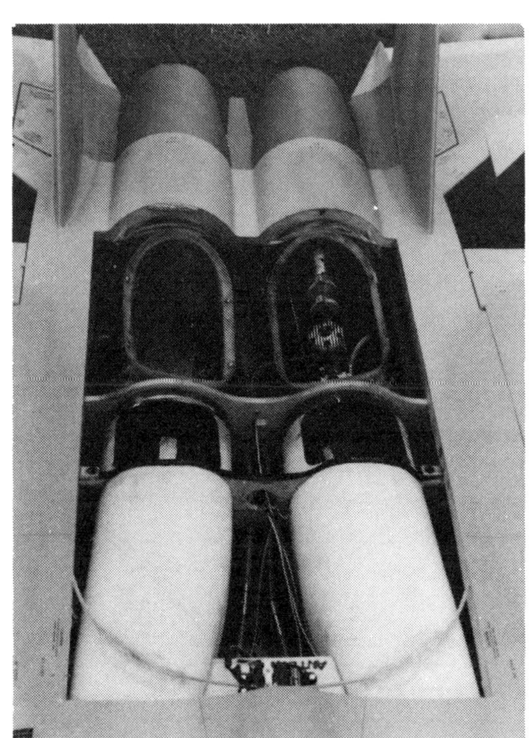

Fig. 5.16.
Examples of
different types of
hatches. (a) Philip
Avond's F-15
Eagle. (b) Ron
Sweeney's F-20
Tigershark.

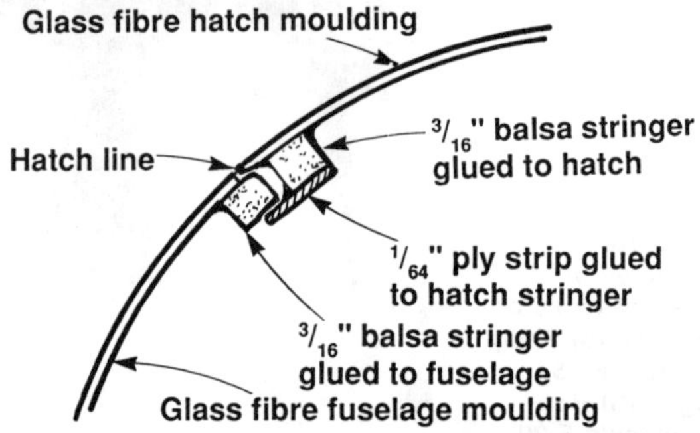

as this maintains the cut edges in close alignment along their entire length. It requires good craftmanship and is retained by springing it into place, usually securing with a latch at one end and dowels at the other.

Chris Golds prefers a hinged hatch (Fig. 5.17 [c]), as it is always there when he wants it. Chris uses a single home-made latch mechanism. The bottle under the hatch contains smoke fluid — not Dutch courage for the pilot!

5.5 Undercarriage

Three choices of undercarriage, or landing gear, are available: retracts, fixed gear, or dispense with it altogether and use a dolly or hand launch. Each option has its merits and demerits.

Taking them in reverse order: the dolly is seldom used for model R/C aircraft other than ducted fans. The reasons for choosing it are cheapness, better performance in air (lower weight and drag), better for grass field landings, and it looks better in flight than fixed u/c. Its disadvantages are that it is not scale, the aircraft may bounce off prematurely, and landings usually cause paint damage. I have found that the dolly can be disguised quite effectively if thoughtfully designed (Fig. 5.18 [a] and [b]), and can even be made to steer while taxiing by attaching a servo to the dolly in such a way that it disconnects from the receiver as the aircraft lifts from the dolly. The tendency to bounce off prematurely can be counteracted by lengthening the horns on the dolly, but this is at the expense of scale appearance. Some modellers have used a servo operated latch mechanism which will only release the dolly when full up-elevator is given.

Fig. 5.18. (a) Dolly for F-86 constructed from ⅛ inch piano wire. (b) The dolly need not be too conspicuous as shown by this ground shot of the F-86.

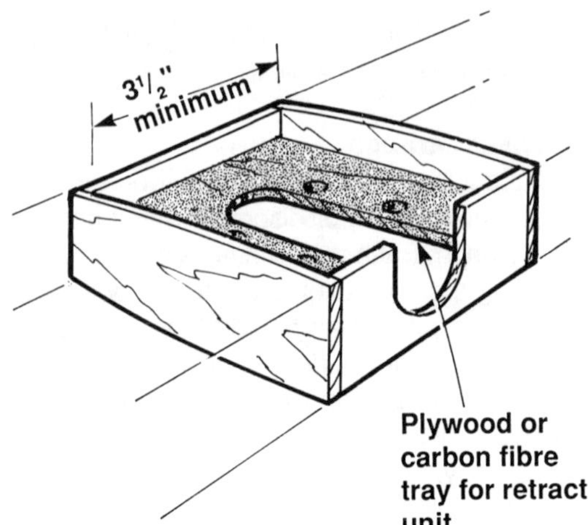

Fig. 5.19. Plywood box housing retracting undercarriage in wing. It should occupy the full wing thickness and be firmly glued to the upper and lower wing skins.

Design of fixed undercarriage is no different from conventional propeller driven aircraft and needs no further explanation. It certainly has its advantages for a ducted fan trainer since, if properly designed, it should be capable of absorbing considerable abuse without damage to the aircraft.

There can be no doubt that a retracting undercarriage is essential if the scale model is to look and behave like the full size aircraft it represents. Fitting retracts follows the same procedures as for conventional aircraft but the following points should be borne in mind. Jets tend to land at higher speeds; this means that the structure needs to absorb impact damage safely. Try to use coiled struts or functioning oleo legs wherever possible. Build a substantial ply box into the wing to house the retracts; 1/16 inch ply is usually adequate but make sure it distributes the landing loads throughout the wing structure. This is particularly important for foam wings; the box should be full depth and firmly bonded to the upper and lower wing skins as well as the foam core (Fig. 5.19). The tray should be strong and *flexible*. Bob Violett advocates the use of carbon fibre reinforced epoxy sheet. This can be quite thin, so that it flexes elastically but remains very strong. Alternatively, 1/8 inch plywood should be quite acceptable, but make the box as large as possible. The plate, with retracts bolted to it, can be manoeuvred in the box until the retract angles are correct and then glued in place. The joints should be reinforced with glass fibre and resin or triangular wood fillets.

A particular problem with the wings on modern jets is that they tend to be very thin. On early jets, the maximum thickness-to-chord ratio was around 0.10 (or 10%). On the F-100 Super Sabre it had de-

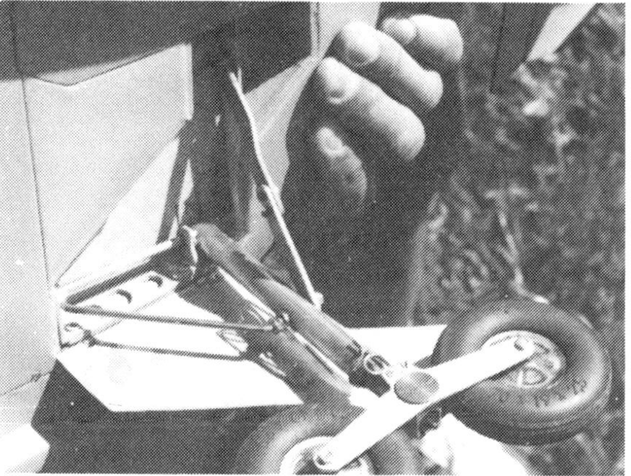

Fig. 5.20. Einar Johnson's ingenious retract units made to fit the very thin wing on his 1:10 scale Saab Viggen.

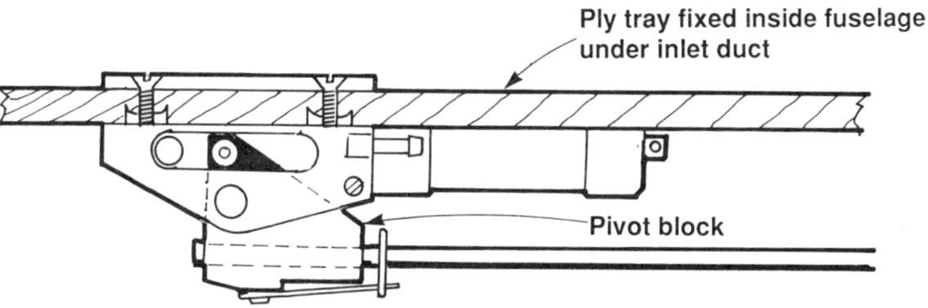

Fig. 5.21. Modifications to ROMAIR nose leg retract mechanism. The depth of the unit is reduced to allow it to fit between the inlet duct and fuselage belly.

creased to 6% and, on the latest jets, typified by the F-16 and F-20, it is around 3%. This could mean a maximum wing thickness of no more than ½ inch for an exact 1:8 scale modern jet. This rules out most commercial retracts which means that special units may have to be built, as for the Saab Viggen shown in Fig. 5.20.

The nose gear retract installation should present no problem for aircraft other than those with nose inlets. Even then, difficulties only arise if full inlet ducting is to be used. Commercial retracts can

Fig. 5.22. A complicated retract problem is posed by the F104 Starfighter. Barry Conway's elegant solution uses modified ROMAIR retracts and features sequencing doors.

Fig. 5.23. Einar Johnson's clever nose gear door mechanism. The piano wire spring should be positioned as far from the nose gear pivot point as practicable.

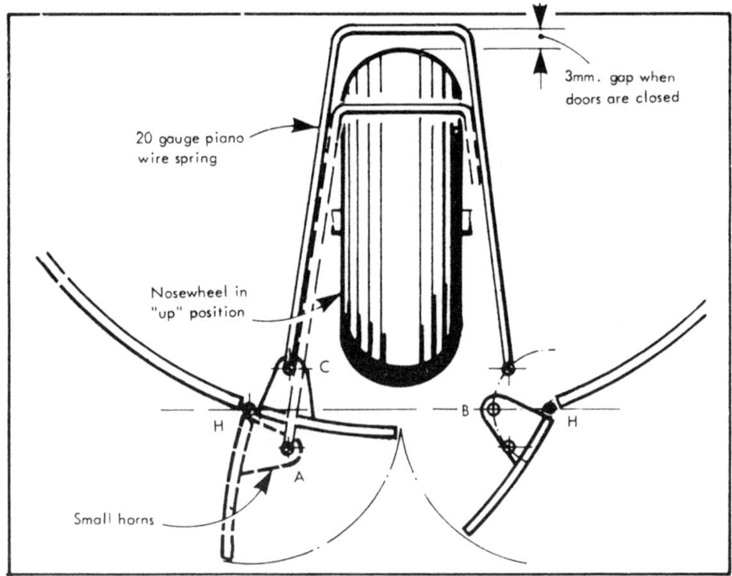

sometimes be modified to produce a 'slimmer' unit. Fig. 5.21 shows how this can be achieved for a standard Romair nose unit. Otherwise, special units will have to be made. The same is true for many of the more complicated undercarriages that retract and twist into the fuselage.

Ideally, the main landing gear location should be about an inch behind the C.G. (with fuel tanks empty if the tanks are in front of the C.G.) If this distance is too small, the nose will tend to bounce up and down in an unrealistic manner while taxiing. If the wheels are too far back, the model may never take off because the elevator authority is insufficient to lift the nose. True, the nose leg can be lengthened and the aircraft 'flown off', but this may destroy the appearance of the aircraft on the ground, unless it is designed for carrier deck use! Either way, the take-off speed must be higher if the undercarriage is moved further back and this is bad news — especially if you fly off grass.

A nose leg that is raked forward, as with many early jets, makes ground handling very difficult unless some castering action can be built in. A tight, or rigid, nose wheel steering linkage helps, but this may not be possible with certain retract units.

Undercarriage doors present further problems unless you happen to be a mechanical masochist (Fig. 5.22). As usual, the main objective is to make the doors reliable but light. Texts written for conventional scale aircraft are generally very helpful but I have included a sketch of a particularly light and elegant solution, devised by a Swedish friend, for a pair of nose doors (Fig. 5.23).

5.6 Ducts

Having decided on the shape of the ducts, particularly inlet and outlet areas, it is then a matter of making and fixing them in place. The ducts can be fixed in place permanently, in which case they can contribute significantly to the strength and stiffness of the fuselage (Fig. 5.24). I prefer to design the whole airframe so that it can be dismantled sufficiently to allow access to all internal components. A single screw is usually adequate to secure the rear duct to the fan shroud. If the duct is made from $\frac{1}{64}$ inch plywood, it should be thoroughly fuel-proofed. Alternative materials are lightweight fibreglass, aluminium litho plate or thin 0.007 inch Lexan plastic sheet. Double-sided adhesive tape can be used to join the seam but an extra layer of normal adhesive tape should be added for extra security.

If the rear duct is not totally impermeable, oil seepage can gradually increase the weight of the aircraft in such a way that the CG moves rearward thus destabilizing the model so that more weight has to be

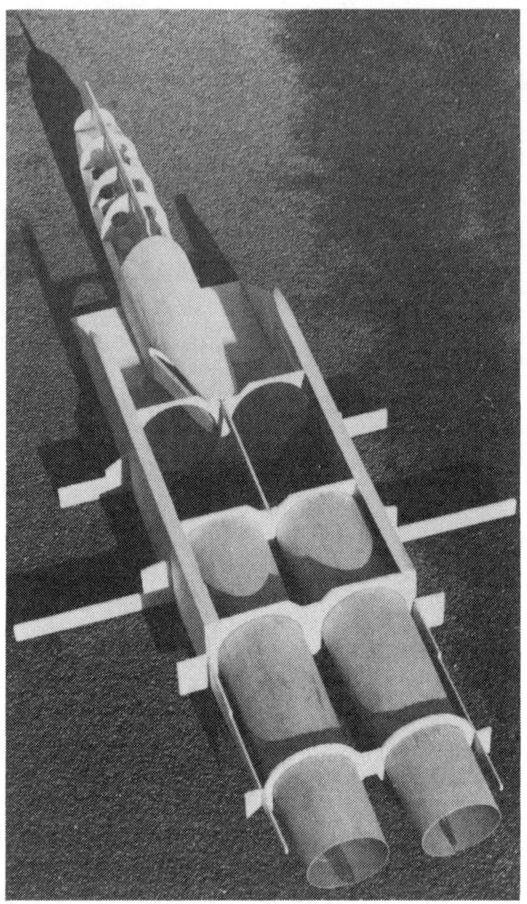

added to the nose to rebalance it. This effect was responsible for a total increase in weight of 12 ounces for one of my models over a five-year period of operation.

The inlet duct needs to be much stiffer to resist its tendency to collapse under the partial vacuum inside it. As stated in Chapter 2, it can be reinforced with stiffening webs or carbon fibre. It is highly desirable to avoid stepped joints where the inlet duct meets the fan shroud, otherwise flow separation can occur with consequent efficiency loss. The spigoted joint shown in Fig. 5.25 works well. The assembly can be easily dismantled if a telescopic joint is introduced further up the inlet duct.

The final requirement is to fit an engine cover cap into the rear duct. This allows access to the engine and tuned pipe connections. A

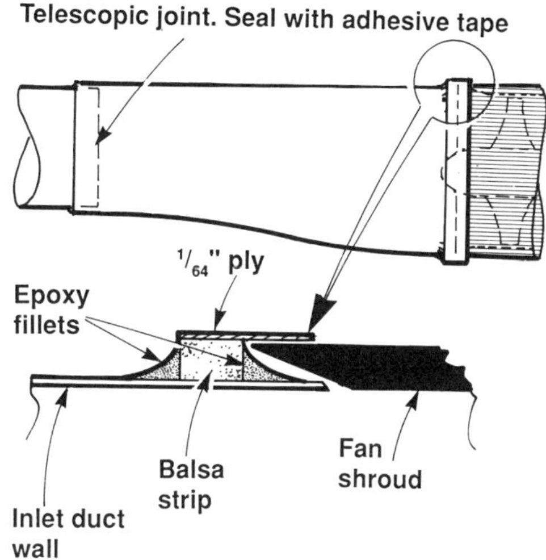

Fig. 5.25. Inlet duct attachment to shroud and telescopic joint (for dismantling) purposes.

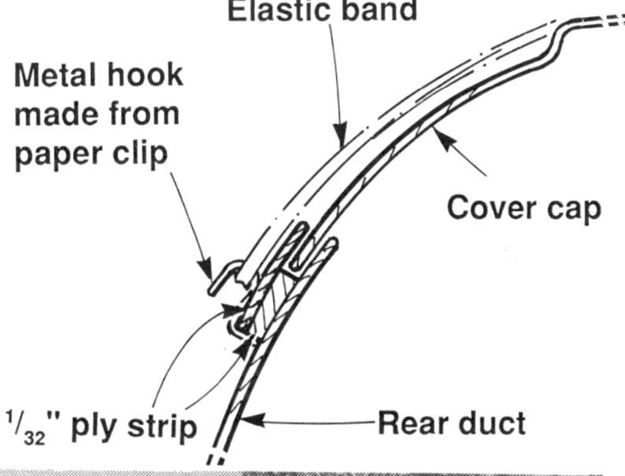

Fig. 5.26. Engine cover cap retention system (a) fitted to Ron Sweeney's F-20 Tigershark (b) Note the neat use of lithoplate to line the inlet duct.

fibreglass cover cap is the usual preference, although a vacuum formed transparent thermoplastic such as Lexan has the advantage that the operator can see through it to monitor the pipe joints, carburettor linkages, fuel tube vibration etc. The cover cap may be held in place by various methods; Philip Avonds uses screws (Fig. 5.16 [a]), Bob Violett used 'O' rings (Fig. 5.17 [a]), others use springs or elastic bands. In the latter case a special 'seat' should be fitted to the duct, so that internal air pressure cannot overcome the tension of the springs or elastic bands and lift the cap. The seat takes the form of a recessed ply frame around the duct cut-out (Fig. 5.26).

Another important function of the cover cap is to direct air around the engine cylinder. It cannot do this effectively if the fit is too close; allow at least ¼ inch clearance all round. If it is carefully shaped, it can also conform to the 'area-ruling' principle outlined in Chapter 2.

5.7 The wing

Wing aerofoil section Earlier parts of this chapter have discussed wing area and loading. Scale requirements may define the shape in terms of planform, but usually even the most devoted of scale modellers will allow himself some latitude with regard to the wing section or aerofoil.

A very thin wing may be essential for a full size mach 2 fighter, in order to overcome compressibility problems near the speed of sound. Such aerofoils generate far less lift than their thicker counterparts and would be quite inappropriate for our relatively slow flying models. They also pose structural problems due to the limited spar depth they can accommodate. As mentioned earlier, fitting of retracts or even servos can be very tricky in a thin wing. Let us therefore accept that compromises are necessary, and select an aerofoil that will allow us to build a structurally sound wing that will not stall above an acceptable landing speed of, say, 30 mph. We should still be able to reach about 150 mph provided an aerofoil is selected that has a reasonably high lift-to-drag ratio and, preferably, a wide drag bucket.

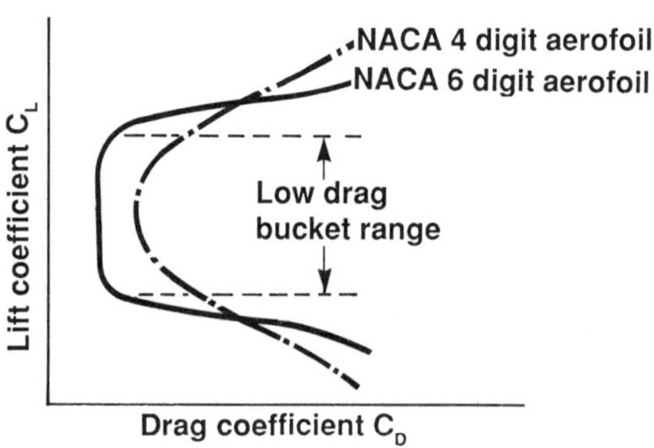

Fig. 5.27. The drag 'bucket'; so called because of its obvious resemblance to a bucket on its side.

Fig. 5.28. NACA 6-figure aerofoil having a drag bucket extending from $c_L = 0$ to $c_L = 0.4$, and a wing maximum thickness of 15% of chord located at the 50% chord position.

Reference to Fig. 5.27 should help to explain these terms; otherwise consult Martin Simons' excellent book *Model Aircraft Aerodynamics*, published by Argus Books, UK.

The 'bottom' of the bucket should be wide and close to the left hand side of the graph. The effect is to give a wide range of angles of attack that will allow the lift to be changed considerably without causing the drag to change appreciably. The NACA aerofoils were introduced during the Second World War and the 6-figure series were widely used on the early jets. They are characterized by having the point of maximum thickness further back from the leading edge than for earlier aerofoils (Fig. 5.28) to preserve laminar flow. In most cases, practice does not live up to the expectations of theory, especially with models, but some genuine benefits are detectable.

As far as model aircraft are concerned, the ducted fan flier can often draw on the experience of model glider enthusiasts. In particular, the sleek slope soarer developed for high penetration in speed events has a lot in common with our model jet. In recent years, such models have moved on from the NACA 6 digit series to Eppler and Wortmann profiles. Generally speaking, a thickness-to-chord ratio of around 12% would seem about right, but deltas and other designs with large root chords could go down to 9%. A semi-symmetrical profile should be best, with a camber that centres the drag bucket at, say $c_L = 0.4$. If the drag bucket extends from $c_L = 0.1$ to $c_L = 0.7$ this should maintain a low drag coefficient for all parts of the normal flight envelope other than on landing finals or very high speed ' pylon' turns. Overcook the latter and, not only is speed lost very rapidly, but you could also experience a 'g' stall with the aircraft flicking out of a turn in a truly disconcerting manner. Early jets had the same problem, this being a key factor in their combat capability.

Tip washout is just as important with jets as with conventional aircraft. A better way to introduce it, rather than by building in a twist of, say 2 or 3°, is to simply increase the camber towards the wing tips.

Wing planform Swept wings were introduced on full size aircraft to counteract compressibility effects as the speed of sound was

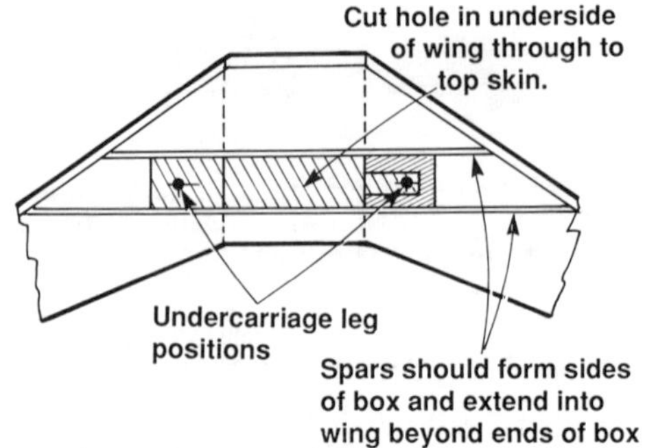

Fig. 5.29. Spar arrangement for swept wings. Front and rear spars should be continuous across the fuselage.

Fig. 5.30. With plug-in wings, the root spars should extend through the fuselage.

approached. No such concern need bother us. However, wing sweep does have three important side effects.

Firstly, it gives a stabilizing effect similar to dihedral. Secondly, lift forces impose a much greater torsional moment to the wing. This must be counteracted by a strong wing skin and spar arrangement. Glass cloth is obviously ideal for the skin. It is best to extend spars right across the fuselage, where possible combining them with retract cut-outs (Fig. 5.29). With mid-wing configurations, stub spars can fit into spar boxes in the wings but, once again, the spar should extend across the fuselage (Fig. 5.30). Judicious use of glass and carbon fibre can be of considerable help without increasing the weight significantly. The problem is even more acute with wings that are swept *forward* because the forces that cause the wing to twist become larger the more the wing twists — an inherently unstable and flutter-prone condition compared to the swept back wing.

The third effect of sweep is to increase the spanwise flow of air (towards the wing tips for sweep back). This impairs wing efficiency and reduces the angle of attack at which the wing will stall. Wing fences are sometimes fitted to reduce the effect. With a swept forward wing the effect is reversed, thus postponing tip stall and allowing safe low-speed handling. High-speed capability should not be changed, provided the wing is stiff enough to prevent twisting.

Leading edge root extensions (LEX) are yet another means for increasing wing lift without affecting drag significantly. Fig. 5.13 shows them fitted to an F-20 Tigershark.

Wing control surfaces Having dealt with most of the fixed features that determine wing behaviour and construction, we will now look at the moveable devices that allow us to control the lift, drag, and stall characteristics of the wing. The wing control surfaces with which modellers are most familiar are the ailerons. These are no different than on conventional models, except that it is more important to seal them so they are effective at small deflections. Large deflections cause increased drag and reduce air speeds. As the air pressure on the surface increases as the square of the airspeed, this means that servo loads at 120 mph can be four times as high as at 60 mph and the servo could stall. If the linkage is too flexible, it might allow the surface to 'blow back' at high speeds.

These considerations apply to all control surfaces but none more so than the flap, due to the large deflections that are required. Just as with full size aircraft, flaps should only be deployed at low speed. If one should get blown back more than the other then a very nasty roll can result. It is worthwhile persevering with flaps because jets are much cleaner (less draggy) than conventional aircraft, especially those having large propellers on the front to act as an airbrake when idling. Without flaps or divebrakes/airbrakes, a ducted fan model can require two circuits to slow down sufficiently for a landing.

Whereas flaps increase lift *and* drag, spoilers are primarily to kill lift and are sometimes used on full size aircraft for roll control, when deployed individually on each wing, and to cause sudden changes in height without a change of pitch or heading, when used simultaneously on each wing. The latter manoeuvre can be particularly useful in combat situations. Divebrakes or airbrakes can be located either on the wing or on the fuselage. Their prime function is to increase drag without reducing lift, although some lift dumping is bound to occur for wing-mounted brakes.

Lift can also be increased by leading edge flaps. On full size aircraft, the flaps (both leading and normal trailing edge types) are used

Fig. 5.31. The swing wing mechanism on a JET AGE F-14 Tomcat built by a group of Belgian modellers.

to change camber and wing area. If the latter operation is to be replicated on a model, some quite sophisticated mechanical engineering is required. More than one model has been written off because flaps did not deploy simultaneously and uniformly. When in doubt, leave them out!

The final, and most demanding, wing control surface mechanism is that of the wing itself, which may be swung backwards or forwards in order to optimise its planform to match the aircraft's speed or operational regime. Several model F-14 Tomcats feature such a mechanism (Fig. 5.31) but difficulties are encountered due to movement of the aerodynamic centre. This tends to make the C.G. too far forward when the wings are fully swept, a problem which the full size aircraft overcomes by pumping fuel back and forth. Also, the primary roll control may change from ailerons to spoilers or to elevons for example. I am not aware of any models utilizing fuel pumps to adjust C.G., but I do know that many of today's P.C.M. Radios are capable of programmable mixing to compensate for the changes in pitch and roll control that occur when almost any of the aforementioned wing control devices are deployed.

Wing Performance More than any other part of the airframe, the wing controls the lift and drag characteristics of the aircraft. That statement is less true today with the advent of 'lifting body' designs but let us

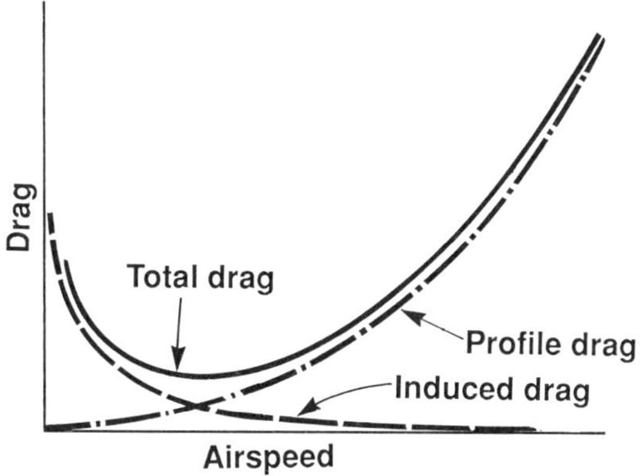

Fig. 5.32.
Derivation of total drag curve from induced drag and profile drag contributions.

accept it for the moment. Several texts indicate how to calculate the total drag of a model aircraft as a function of airspeed but Martin Simons' *Model Aircraft Aerodynamics* (Argus Books) is probably one of the best. Basically, the total drag is made up of three components:

1) *Induced drag* is generated by the lifting function of the wing. As speed increases, angle of attack decreases and so does induced drag. Induced drag is therefore very high at low speeds and very small at high speeds (Fig. 5.32).

2) *Profile drag* is due to pressure variations as air is forced to flow around a body, combined with the friction of the air flowing over the surface. This type of drag increases as the square power of air speed (Fig. 5.32).

3) *Parasite drag* is due to any part of the aircraft surface that does not contribute to lift and is not perfectly streamlined. Protruberances such as cockpits, intakes, fairings etc. all contribute to parasite drag. It also increases with increase in airspeed.

If these contributions are added to give the total drag, a curve of the form shown in Fig. 5.32 results.

Such a curve has been calculated for an approximate 1:8 scale model jet weighing 7.6 pounds with a wing area of 640 square inches using the NACA 65_3412 aerofoil, Fig. 5.33. Also shown on this graph is the dynamic thrust curve estimated for the same plane fitted with a fan unit giving 7.6 pounds of static thrust. Fig. 5.33 can yield a lot of useful information if used in conjunction with Fig. 5.34 which describes the forces acting on an aircraft climbing at an angle of $\theta°$. Resolving the forces in such a way as to eliminate lift gives

$$T - D = W \sin \theta$$

or, $$\sin \theta = \frac{T-D}{W} \qquad (10)$$

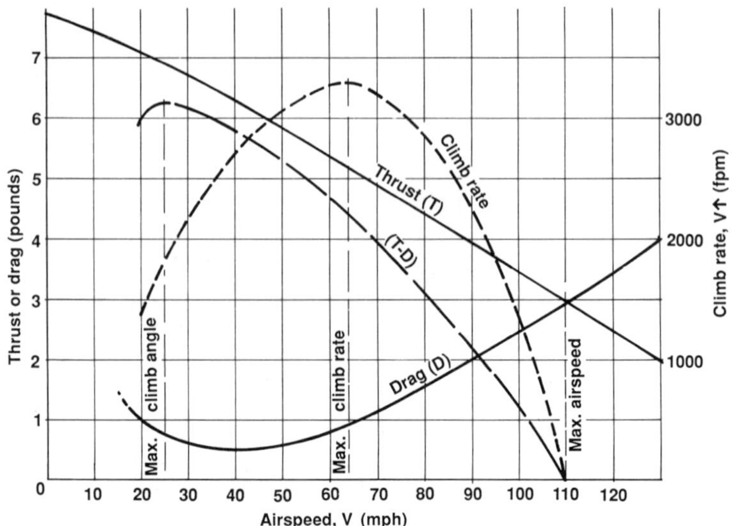

Fig. 5.33. Thrust, drag and performance curves for a 1:8 scale model jet weighing 7.6 pounds, wing area 640 square inches, NACA 65$_3$412 aerofoil, static thrust 7.8 pounds.

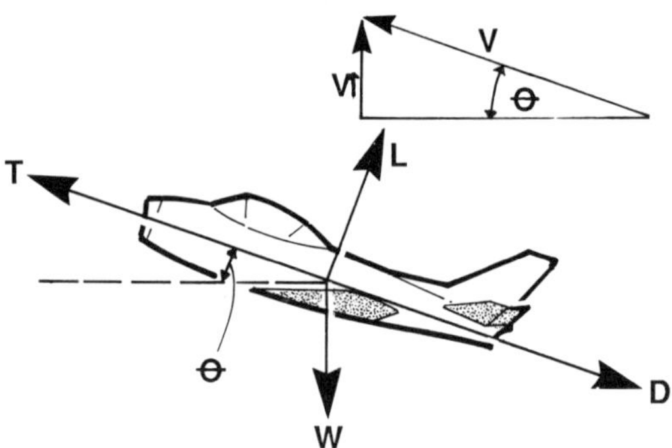

Fig. 5.34. Forces acting on an aircraft climbing at an angle of θ°. T = Thrust, D = Drag, L = Lift, W = Weight. Inset figure shows velocity relationships where V is the air speed and V↑ is the vertical climb rate.

In other words, the climb angle will be greatest when T-D is at its maximum. The T-D curve is obtained by subtracting the drag curve from the thrust curve in Fig. 5.33 to produce the broken line. This passes through a maximum at 25 mph corresponding to a value of T-D = 6.3 pounds. Substituting this figure in Equation (10) gives a maximum climb angle of θ = 55°. This may surprise some readers because the Thrust-to-Weight ratio is greater than unity (^{T}/w = 7.8/ 7.6 = 1.03) thus it might be supposed that the aircraft would fly straight up indefinitely. What happens is that the flying speed falls below the stall condition and control is lost unless the aircraft is fitted with stabilizing devices such as the vectored thrust nozzles fitted to rockets and V.T.O. aircraft.

The T-D curve passes through zero pounds at an airspeed of 110 mph when thrust is exactly balanced by drag in level flight and there is no motive force left to accelerate the aircraft further.

Fig. 5.34 also shows the relationship between airspeed, V, and climb rate V↑(or the rates at which the aircraft gains altitude)

$$V\uparrow = V \sin \theta$$

From equation (10) (10)

$$\sin \theta = \frac{T - D}{W}$$

Therefore $V\uparrow = \frac{V (T - D)}{W}$ (11)

The climb rate, V↑can be calculated easily by reading off values of V and T-D from Fig. 5.33. We can then plot V↑as the dotted line on the same graph by putting climb rate (in feet per minute) on the right hand scale. Climb rate starts at zero while the aircraft is on the ground just before rotation, and returns to zero when the aircraft reaches 110 mph which is the maximum speed in level flight. In between, V↑ reaches a maximum value of 3300 feet per minute at an airspeed of 64 mph. Note that this occurs at a higher airspeed than the maximum climb angle. In fact, maximum climb rate coincides with a climb angle of $\theta = 35°$. These happen to be very respectable climb angles and rates compared with the actual performance figures for full size private and commercial aircraft. In *scale* terms, the climb angle, climb rate and maximum speed give a good representation of one of the early supersonic aircraft such as the Hawker Hunter or F-100D Super Sabre. The stalling speed (around 25 mph) is a little on the high side but scale performance realism is possible with a ducted fan aircraft to an extent that is generally out of the question with most conventional propeller-driven aircraft. This fact is not lost on judges at scale competitions.

A final observation from Fig. 5.33 is that the minimum drag occurs at around 40 mph. At this airspeed, the thrust need only be around ½ pound to maintain level flight (a thrust-to-weight ratio of less than 0.1!) This is the reason why model jets really do need devices such as flaps and airbrakes to increase drag, otherwise they seem to glide forever before slowing down to a safe landing speed. Reference back to Chapter 2 and Fig. 3.13 shows that a THORJET fan, for example, will still produce ½ pound of thrust at 6,100 rpm. In fact, the engine must be capable of safe idling below 4,000 rpm if the aircraft is ever going to slow down to 30 mph without flaps etc. This would be easy to achieve if the engine was turning a large propeller but is, actually, quite demanding for a small diameter, low inertia impeller. If all else fails (no flaps, brakes and rpm too high) take a leaf out of the glider pilot's book and try side-slipping to increase profile drag.

In summary, Fig. 5.33 gives an interesting indication of what to *expect* from a model jet. These expectations can be compared with roughly measured values of climb angle (judged by eye) and maximum airspeed (timed over a known distance). Maximum climb rate is a little more difficult — I will leave that to the more ingenious readers! Of greater value, perhaps, is the way that Fig. 5.33 can be interpreted to indicate ways of improving the performance of our models. Clearly, static thrust largely determines maximum climb angle because the actual airspeed is low (about 30 mph). Dynamic thrust is more important in determining maximum climb rate, and is absolutely crucial to maximum airspeed. The other factor that fixes the maximum airspeed is drag. At high speed the induced drag is negligible and only the profile and parasitic drag need concern us. They contribute roughly equal amounts to the total calculated drag at 110 mph, therefore careful attention to surface finish, streamlined fairings, wheel doors, trailing edges, intake lips etc. should be repaid by higher flight speeds. The level of improvement to expect, however, will be comparatively modest. Fig. 5.33 shows that, if the drag is halved or the dynamic thrust doubled, we can only expect an increase of 20 mph in maximum airspeed in level flight. An increase in wing loading may well produce higher diving speeds but that depends on the choice of aerofoil.

5.8 The empennage

The empennage includes all flying surfaces other than the wing, i.e. the vertical and horizontal stabilizers (fin and tailplane or canard).

The fin Determination of fin size must take into account the dihedral angle and the wing sweep, which contributes a dihedral effect. If the fin is too small, lateral stability is reduced and a Dutch roll may result. Too large a fin may cause spiral instability leading to an uncontrollable spiral dive. There are no simple design rules to go by other than to replicate the fin size and shape of a similar model of full size aircraft, then observe your creation in flight and adjust fin size, dihedral or wing sweep as necessary. I once noticed a curious 'shimmy' in a model. It was not sufficient to be called a Dutch roll as the tail only weathercocked through a small angle with very little tendency to roll.

Fig. 5.35. The all-flying tail (a) compared with a conventional tailplane and elevator (b).

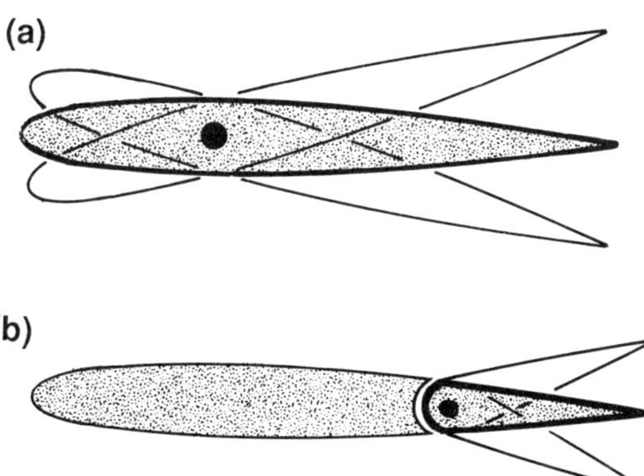

The effect was most noticeable in gusty weather or when pulling out of a tight turn. I reasoned that a larger fin was needed, but a friend with full size experience suggested that I should simply increase the thickness of the trailing edge on the rudder. This corrected the shimmy, presumably by increasing the effectiveness, or power, of the fin and rudder at the expense of a little extra drag.

In many ducted fan models a little weight can be saved by dispensing with the rudder as a control surface as it is so seldom used in flight. With full size fighters, it mainly serves to align the aircraft for gunnery purposes and for crosswind take-offs and landings. The rudder is, of course, essential for knife edge flight and useful for drag-increase, side-slipping manoeuvres.

The tailplane Tailplane size, shape and location is closely related to centre of gravity and centre of pressure, as discussed at the beginning of this chapter. In modern jets there is a tendency to favour the all-flying tailplane rather than the more familiar tailplane fitted with an elevator (Fig. 5.35). Among modellers, there seems to be a misconception that all-flying tails need only move through a small angle to be as effective as a normal tailplane with elevators. This is simply not so, as observation of a full size Tornado, Phantom or Tomcat on take-off will confirm. A deflection range of + 20° to - 40° is quite typical. On all-flying tailplanes fitted to earlier jets the range was smaller, but the tailplane movement was mechanically coupled to an elevator thereby increasing its effectiveness or authority.

All-flying tailplanes can pose structural problems, in that the pivot usually has to pass through the fuselage. Some form of yoke is necessary, to which each half of the tailplane is firmly secured. Fig. 5.36 shows an example that can be adapted to many prototypes if the wires connecting the two halves are shaped to pass around the rear

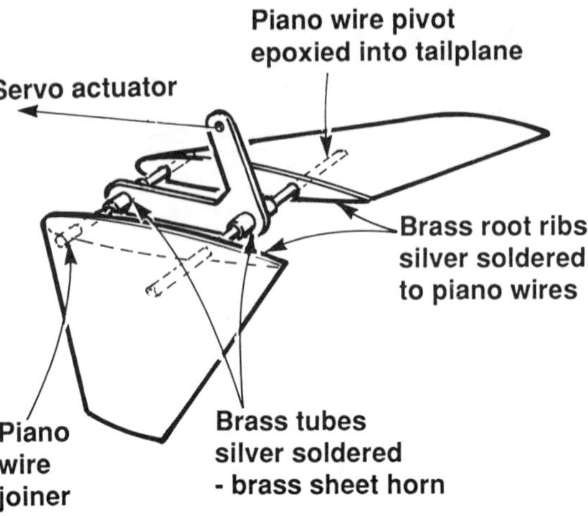

Fig. 5.36. All-flying tailplane yoke fabricated from brass sheet and piano wire. The two piano wires are cut in the middle before the horn is fitted. This is accomplished after the two half-tailplanes are placed in position on the fuselage. The brass tubes are then soft-soldered to the piano wires thus re-joining the two half-tailplanes.

duct. All flying tailplanes are also prone to flutter. A long elevator horn helps but the problem can be avoided altogether if the tailplane is mass-balanced. The completed assembly should be supported by placing the pivot rod on a knife edge. Weight is then added to the leading edge until it is nose heavy. In other words, the C.G. of the tailplane must lie in front of the pivot axis if flutter is to be avoided. The same maxim can be applied to all control surfaces.

The tailplane may be quite large on certain designs and could therefore be capable of exerting very large forces on the servo. Fortunately, this problem is easily overcome by placing the pivot point 25% back from the leading edge at the mean aerodynamic chord (see Fig. 5.7). This is called 'aerodynamic balancing' and should reduce the tailplane pitching moment and, hence, servo loads to a very low level.

Tailplane authority is of greatest importance during take-off when it is required to provide a rotational force to lift the nose and give the wing a suitable angle of attack to generate the lift necessary for flight. An indication of the force the tailplane has to exert can be obtained by setting the plane on a level surface and then placing weights on the tailplane until the aircraft tilts back on its main wheels. As a very rough guide, the added weight should be no more than 5% of the total weight of the aircraft. A more accurate figure can be obtained from a knowledge of the tailplane moment arm and aerodynamic loading. If the tailplane authority is insufficient to cause rotation, this can be corrected either by moving the main legs forward a little or by length-ening the nose leg so that the wing has a small positive angle of

Fig. 5.37. Jet Canard configuration exemplified by the Saab Viggen displayed here by its proud Swedish owner Einar Johnson.

incidence with respect to the ground.

If the tailplane is placed high on the fin, a phenomenon known as 'deep stall' can occur at high angles of attack, during a landing approach for example. As the aircraft approaches stalling speed the tailplane becomes 'blanketed' by the wing, loses authority and cannot apply sufficient corrective force to bring the nose down. The nose then pitches up more dramatically and airspeed is lost as the aircraft descends vertically. Several T-tail jet transports exhibited this problem, as did the Gloster Javelin. The cure is either to move the tailplane out of the blanketed area or improve stability (avoid the stall) by moving the C.G. forward.

The Canard This arrangement of flying surfaces, popularised by the Saab Viggen (Fig. 5.37) is now very much in vogue for the latest fashion-conscious generation of fighters. The canard, or foreplane, acts as a horizontal stabilizer just as the tailplane does but it is designed to stall *before* the mainplane thus lowering the nose of the aircraft in a safe manner as the stall is approached. It also serves to direct the flow of air over the mainplane in such a way as to reduce its angle of attack and delay the stall.

If fitted with a control surface, the canard can act as an elevator, or, in the case of the Viggen, as a flap which allows an even higher angle of attack to be achieved thus shortening take off and landing runs.

Finally, the canard can be made all-flying as with the new European Advanced Fighter (EAF). Its primary function then is to trim the aircraft so that the mainplane (or wing) is always operating under optimum conditions. When the aircraft has landed, the canard can be tilted

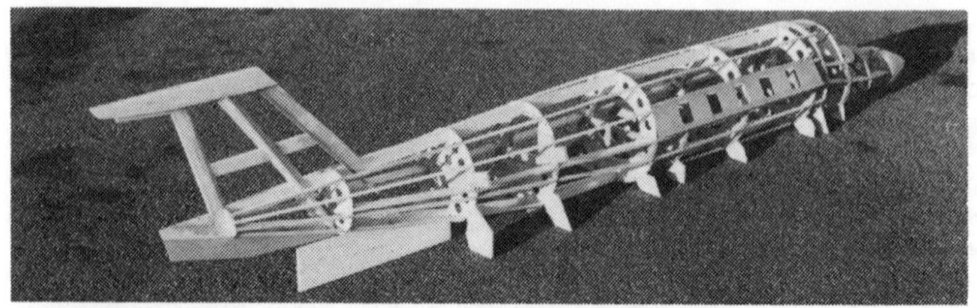

Fig. 5.38. Built-up wooden structures are still popular with scratch builders.

downwards at almost 90° to act as an airbrake and shorten the landing run.

5.9 Materials, construction and finishing techniques

There is little doubt that the complex aerodynamic shapes of jet aircraft are well suited to fibreglass moulding techniques. The built-up wooden structure still survives and works well for scratchbuilders and those working from plans (Fig. 5.38) but most kit manufacturers supply fibreglass fuselages. Although such structures appear quite simple, a great deal of thought and time goes into their fabrication. Consider, for example, the polyester resin, glass-fibre reinforced fuselage of a Turbofan F-86 Sabre. The bulk of the fuselage is made from two layers of woven glass cloth reinforced by additional glass tapes at the 3, 6, 9 and 12 o'clock positions. The wing seat, inlet and outlet holes are further reinforced by individual glass fibres (or rovings) as are other areas where hatches are to be cut. The fin is made from chopped strand matt because strength takes second place to shape here, and a woven cloth fin would tend to distort after removal from the mould. The very high standard of surface finish and absence of pinholes requires the minimum of preparation prior to painting.

The glass fibre-to-resin weight ratio should be as high as possible, provided that all fibres are wetted by the resin. Epoxy resins are generally better than polyester resins from this point of view thus making lighter, stronger, fuselages possible. Unfortunately, this advantage is often lost because the number of pinholes is higher than for polyester resin thus requiring application of a paste filler. Generally speaking, fibreglass fuselages provided by ducted fan kit manufacturers are clear due to the high weight buildup with pigmented resins.

The trick is to introduce strength and stiffness only where it is required. This has become much easier with the advent of very strong, light reinforcing materials, such as Kevlar and graphite. We

Fig. 5.39. Glass fibre wing skins give an excellent representation of metal. Note use of shadowing to give the impression of a flap.

have already seen how these materials can be used to stiffen ducts, to produce flexible plates on which to mount undercarriages and to strengthen spars. I have also used small strips of carbon fibre to stiffen the entire tail area of an aircraft that was observed to twist and flutter in flight.

Glass fibre can also be used in the form of a lightweight cloth to give an excellent skinning material for wooden surfaces. When filled and abraded to a smooth finish it provides a high strength damage-resistant surface that gives the appearance of metal when painted (Fig. 5.39).

Fig. 5.40. Chris Golds' 14ft, four-fan Concorde — all foam and brown paper!

Fig. 5.41. Vacuum formed styrene moldings can be used to produce a convincing cockpit interior without increasing weight by more than 1½ ounces.

Low density polystyrene foam is as popular for ducted fan kits as it is with other power model and glider kits. Careful manufacture can ensure that complex aerofoil sections are accurately reproduced. Foam is also being used with remarkable success by a few talented pioneers, as a structural material for fuselages. When covered with brown paper and wallpaper paste it can be finished like any other surface. Chris Golds' enormous 14-foot long Concorde illustrates what can be achieved by this method (Fig. 5.40).

Vacuum-formed accessories are very common for all sorts of add-on features such as bubbles, blisters, guns, inlets, fairings, canopies etc. Vacuum formings from very thin styrene can also be used for detailing cockpit interiors. Cockpit interiors look so much better when they appear to have some depth and detail (Fig. 5.41).

Because very little fuel residue is deposited on the finished surfaces, there is generally no need to fuel-proof ducted fan models other than around the tailpipe outlet. Beware of splashing high nitro fuel onto the paintwork, however.

6 AUXILIARY SYSTEMS

Having dealt with the airframe and power plant of a ducted fan model it is now necessary to consider fuel management and radio control. This chapter will conclude with a review of a whole range of optional systems (gimmicks!)

6.1 The fuel supply system

Ducted fans tend to be fuel-guzzling machines: a large twin fan model might consume up to 3 pounds of fuel in a single flight. Add to that the effects of sustained high-g manoeuvres, generally higher vibration levels and large carburettor venturis with little natural suction, and you have a fuel system that is much more demanding than for most sports-type power models.

The high rate of fuel flow is not much of a problem provided that the smallest bore fuel tubing is avoided. Delivery of fuel at the correct rate for the engine (neither too much nor too little for all flight conditions) is more difficult. The mixture needle and carburettor throttle act as metering devices, of course, but they do depend on the pressure of the fuel delivered to the carburettor being kept within a certain range.

Byron Originals tackles the problem by maintaining a constant head of fuel in the second of two tanks, using a chicken hopper principle (Fig. 6.1). The first tank is pressurized by the tuned pipe and the second (header) tank is situated approximately on the centre line of the carburettor.

The tuned pipe is usually capable of supplying more than enough pressure to lift the fuel to the carburettor no matter what the attitude of the aircraft. Furthermore, it also meters the fuel, to a limited extent, because pipe pressure is determined by engine speed. Usually, however, the response time is too long to cope with rapid changes in fuel demand. Section 4.2 covered the relative merits of tuned pipe versus fuel pump systems and concluded that the fuel pump was generally not necessary. Some pumps are fitted with special metering

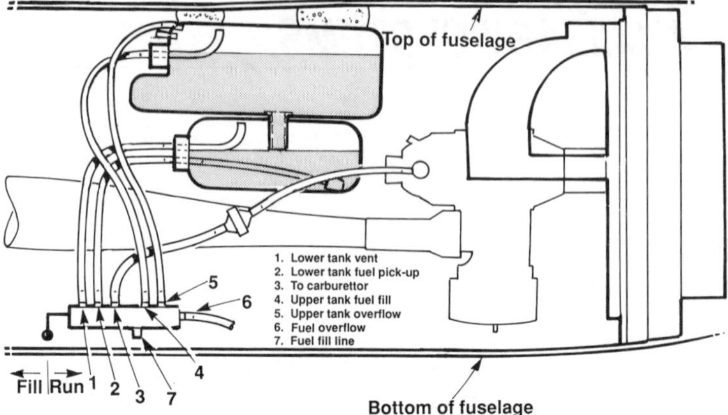

Fig. 6.1. Byron Originals 'SURE-FLOW' fuel tank system maintains a constant head of fuel at the level of the carburettor needle.

Fig. 6.2. The remote needle valve fitted to a VIOJETT allows safe and convenient adjustment of fuel mixture. The photo also shows a carbon fibre reinforced inlet duct and twin tank fuel system that is connected 'in parallel'.

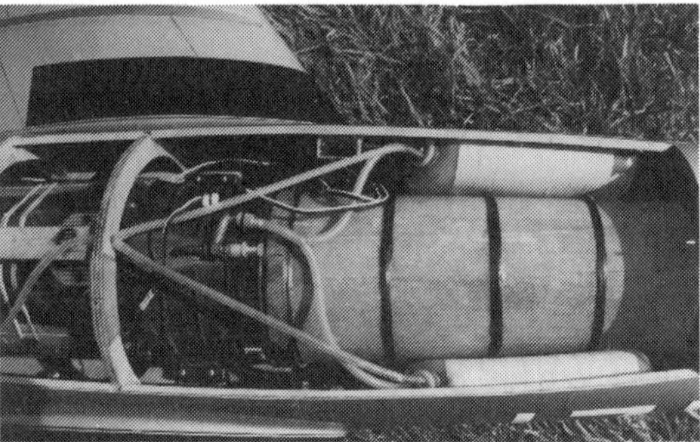

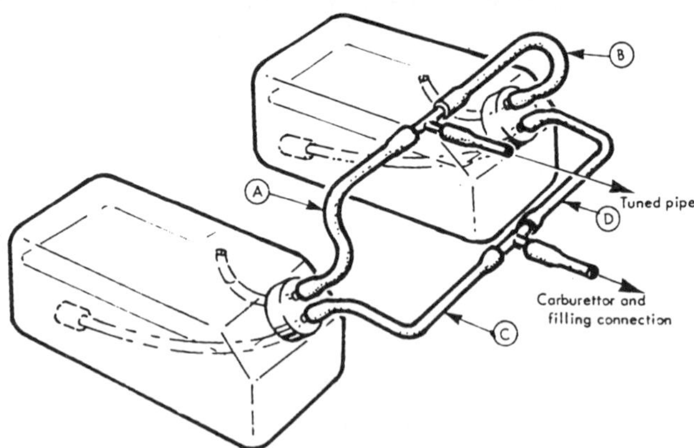

Fig. 6.3. Plumbing diagram for two fuel tanks connected to a single engine. Tubes 'C' and 'D' should be the same diameter and length. Same goes for tubes 'A' and 'B'.

adjustments and these may be worth a closer look, but make sure that they do not cease to function when engine rpm rises above a certain level, or when the fuel demand is too great. Whatever system is used, it must be reliable.

Section 4.2 also dealt with the consequences and prevention of problems with tuned pipes used as fuel pressure devices. Fitting an in-flight-mixture-control is a useful insurance against trouble. It is simply a modification that allows the normal needle valve to be connected to a servo thus allowing it to be adjusted from the radio transmitter. It also provides a safe way to adjust the needle valve after the engine has been started. If such a facility is not available, a remote needle valve is strongly recommended as a convenient and safe way of adjusting the fuel mixture. The VIOJETT is fitted with one as standard (Fig. 6.2) but OS engines also supply a suitable needle valve (Part No. 228 819 00). If the remote needle valve is suspended between rubber cushions, there should be no likelihood of vibration-induced needle wear that sometimes occurs when the needle is part of the carburettor.

If two tanks supply one engine they should be connected in parallel, (Figs. 6.2 and 6.3) not in series, so as to avoid the sudden change in fuel flow when the first tank empties. For many fuselages, especially those with nose inlets, there is very little space in which to fit the fuel tank(s). The oval section 'Pylon Band' fuel tanks manufactured by Sullivan are very useful in this respect and can also be fitted in wings. Very recently, Bob Violett Models have produced a 'fuel cell' specially contoured to fit the space between the duct and fuselage (Fig. 6.4).

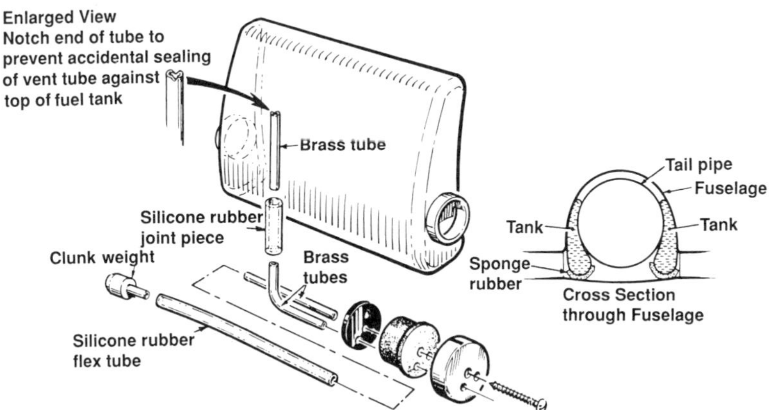

Fig. 6.4. Bob Violett Models 'fuel cell' is specially contoured to fit between the duct and fuselage side.

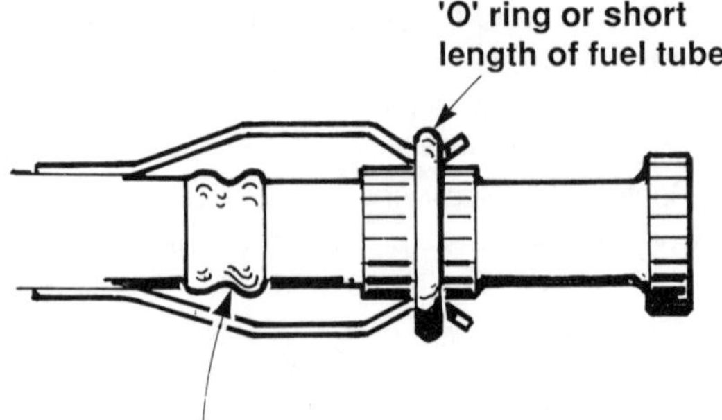

Fig. 6.5. Simple method to prevent needle valve turning due to vibration. Air in-leakage is also minimized.

I have stated that the fuel supply must be absolutely reliable if lean runs and engine cuts are to be avoided. Apart from using a pumping or pressurising system that maintains a roughly constant head, there are several other factors to consider. If the fuel lines or tank are not properly supported and isolated from vibration, cavitation can occur leading to bubbles, rather than fuel, being delivered to the carburettor. Vibration can also cause the needle valve to close. This can be cured by increasing pressure on the ratchet mechanism that is used to stop the needle valve from rotating. A short piece of fuel tube between the needle and the needle housing also helps to stop needle movement and has the secondary advantage of preventing air in-leakage at this point (Fig. 6.5). It should go without saying that dirt in the fuel could cause a lean run if it reached the carburettor. Good fuel filters should always be used between the tank and the carburettor and when filling the tanks.

As a final safeguard against the consequences of a lean run, there is no doubt in my mind that castor oil is a necessary ingredient of any ducted fan fuel. It is true that power increases can often be obtained with fuels based on synthetic oils but this is usually because the total oil content is reduced. That extra 500 rpm is often achieved at the cost of engine lifetime.

6.2 The radio control system

The only ways in which ducted fans differ from conventional models, with regard to the radio control system, are related to: 1) available space 2) vibration levels 3) servo loads, and 4) possible mixing requirements.

The space problem is generally easier to solve for models that have

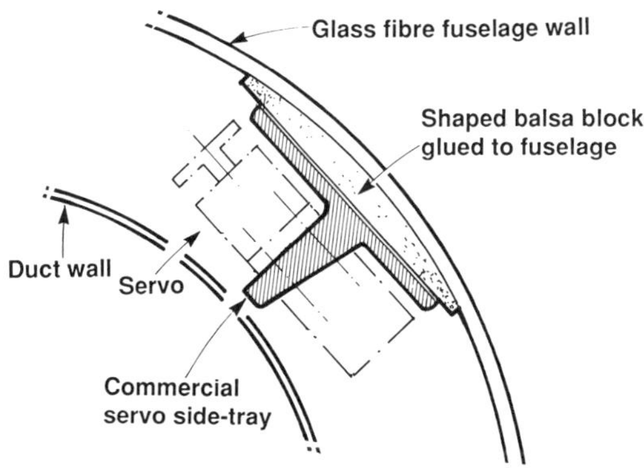

Fig. 6.6. Arrangement for fitting a servo between duct and fuselage. Abrade the fuselage wall before gluing the balsa block in place. Use silicon rubber adhesive between balsa and servo tray.

cheek or chin inlets, as the servos can be placed in the nose (Fig. 5.4). For models with nose inlets, the servos have to be located between the duct and the fuselage wall. Servos mounted in 'side-trays' are ideal for this purpose, but care must be taken that they are absolutely secure. A fixing method for a glass fibre fuselage is shown in Fig. 6.6.

Rigid push rod arrangements are usually impossible in ducted fan fuselages, due to shape and space constraints. Flexible nylon 'snakes' linkages are acceptable but they must be secured every few inches along their length. A reduction in 'slop' can be achieved by gluing a length of steel wire or cable inside the hole in the inner nylon rod.

The radio receiver aerial can be placed inside the fuselage but it should be restrained from too much movement and kept as straight as possible. The outer sheath of a nylon 'nyrod' fixed to the fuselage wall provides a convenient way of housing the aerial and allows it to be removed and re-threaded very easily.

Vibration can cause rapid wear of servo potentiometer contacts, fatigue failure of electrical wiring, damage to drive gears, and electrical noise. All the usual methods should be employed to isolate the radio gear from vibration, but a better approach is to try to isolate the source of vibration from the airframe. Fig. 6.7 shows a shock-absorbing system for attaching the fan and engine assembly to the

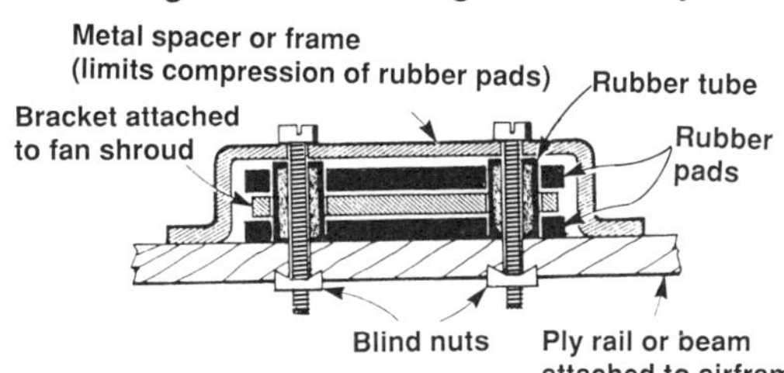

Fig. 6.7. Fan/engine mounting system developed for the VIOJETT minimizes transmission of vibration to the airframe.

airframe. It is similar to that used on the VIOJETT fan.

The high speeds of ducted fan aircraft can impose high loads on servos and linkages. One obvious cure is to use powerful servos and short stiff linkages wherever possible. Some redundancy should be built in to the most critical controls (elevator and aileron). Employ two servos for each function when possible and use aerodynamic balancing to reduce servo loads, as described in Section 5.8.

Some of the more complex ducted fan aircraft contain a large number of servos, so battery drain can be quite rapid. Large batteries and back-up systems should be carefully considered from the point of view of safe flying. Long servo leads should contain electrical noise suppressors. Any electric motors driving retracts or other systems should be checked for possible interference with the radio. Make sure that all servo leads and other wiring is secure and neatly tied down.

6.3 Optional systems

These are add-on options, not necessary for flight but quite impressive at displays and in front of judges at scale competitions. Remember that they are further things to go wrong in models that are already quite complicated. This isn't crucial if it is simply a matter of a strobe light failing, but if a drogue chute deploys in flight the consequences could be serious! We should therefore ensure that the optional systems are engineered to as high a standard as the rest of the aircraft.

The preceding chapter dealt with retracts, wheel doors, and various forms of control surface (flaps, airbrakes, spoilers, swing wings, canards etc.) so I will not discuss them further in this section.

Wheel brakes These can be a particularly useful option on a ducted fan as they allow the aircraft to taxi out and line up for take-off, then, with the brakes applied, run up to almost full throttle thus clearing the engines of excess fuel before releasing the brakes with every confidence that the engines will not flame out. As jets have higher landing speeds than other aircraft, they can quite easily run off the average club strip unless some form of braking is applied. The brake is usually actuated by the elevator servo in the full down position. A single nose wheel brake can be of some use but a better arrangement is to have brakes on both main wheels. The brake should not be capable of locking the wheels. If it can hold the aircraft at around 75% of full rpm that should be sufficient. Mechanical brakes are quite acceptable but pneumatic brakes provide a reliable scale-like alternative (Fig. 6.8). If the main wheel brakes are connected to the

Fig. 6.8. TURBOFAN pneumatic brakes fitted to both main wheels reduce landing runs and allow the engines to run up to 75% rpm before take-off.

Fig. 6.9. Engines on twins should be inclined at 45° to minimize sympathetic vibration as on Reg Smith's Foxbat.

rudder servo they can be applied differentially for taxiing and parking.

Multi-engines These are not strictly an option, although it is quite often possible to simulate full size twins like the Phantom, Lightning or Javelin by a single fan in a model. There are no special rules that apply to ducted fan twins, other than to incline the engines at 45° in order to minimize the problem of sympathetic engine vibration (Fig. 6.9).

Drop tanks and bombs Such external stores certainly help to dress up a model but can cause a lot of drag when airborne (Fig. 6.10). Commercial bomb releases work well but drop tank release mechanisms need careful thought; if one drops and the other doesn't, landing can be tricky. It is best to keep the final turn and touchdown faster than usual. Provided the geometry used on the full size version

Fig. 6.10. Sabre fitted with drop tanks. Make sure the release mechanism is reliable before flying.

Fig. 6.11. Chris Golds' 18 pound BYROJET-powered Hunter heavily ladened with stores. Chris is experimenting with real rockets! Note also the drogue chute doors just above the tailpipe.

is replicated on the model there should be no problem with the tanks lifting and hitting the tailplane.

Rockets I have seen a videotape of successful in-flight rocket launches but have no firsthand experience. Chris Golds is experimenting with his Hawker Hunter (Fig. 6.11). Although the rocket may fire successfully every time on the ground, the air pressure at high speed can be sufficient to prevent the rocket leaving its launcher.

Drogue parachute This never fails to wow the crowd! Bob Fiorenze's Phantom must have gathered plenty of competition points this way. The 'chute can also serve a genuinely useful function on short runways. Close examination of the Hunter in Fig. 6.11 reveals the doors of the 'chute box just above the tailpipe.

Opening canopy This seemed the ultimate in sophistication when demonstrated on Larry Wolfe's Mirage at Abingdon in 1982. Since then it has become a feature of many fine models including the large Byron Eagle shown in Fig. 6.12. There must be no possibility of the

Fig. 6.12. Canopy release mechanism opens remotely on Mark Frankel's Byron Eagle. Model flies well with 2 BYROJETS and ROSSI-81 engines.

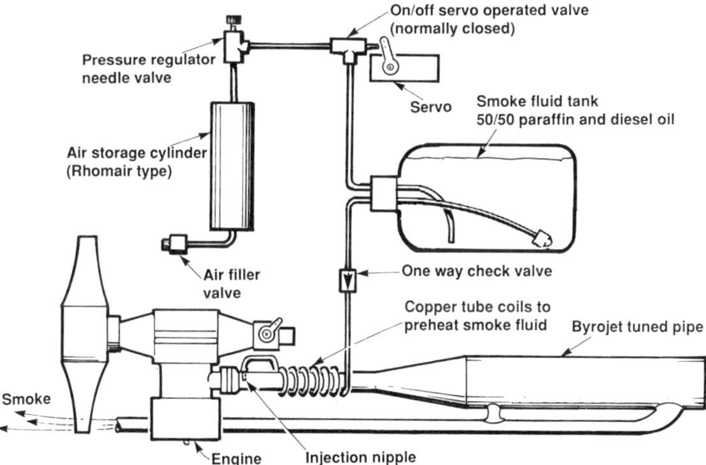

Fig. 6.13. Smoke system shown fitted to a BYROJET ducted fan. The arrangement could be easily adapted to a normal tractor fan installation.

release mechanism operating while the aircraft is in flight.

Smoke system This is another attractive option for flying displays. The arrangement shown in Fig. 6.13 was developed by Harry Woods in California for his Byron F-16. I have also used it many times and found it to be very reliable. The smoke fluid can be paraffin, kerosene (diesel) or a mixture of the two. All tubing should be urethane hose; silicone tube swells and softens rapidly and neoprene is not much

Fig. 6.14. (a)Alec Cornish-Trestrail's Viggen in reverse thrust mode.

(b) This is how it is done. A horizontal vane across the tailpipe can be rotated through 90°.

better. The copper pre-heater coil can be omitted without a major effect on the smoke plume. As smoke fluid enters the tuned pipe it increases the back pressure in the pipe and causes the engine to run rich for a few seconds. Fig. 5.17 (c) shows a smoke system installed in Chris Golds' Hunter.

Reverse thrust Fig. 6.14 (a) may be mistaken for a smoke system being operated on the ground but it is actually Alec Cornish-Trestrail's Viggen being reversed into the pits! Alec uses a horizontal vane placed across the tailpipe (Fig. 6.14 [b]), which can be rotated through almost 90°, like a butterfly valve, to divert the flow forwards and out through the scale vents in the fuselage sides.

Chris Golds' futuristic 'Skywolf' uses a different mechanism based

Fig. 6.15. Eyelid thrust reverser mechanism on Chris Golds' Skywolf.

on the 'eyelid' principle (Fig. 6.15).

A thrust reverser is far more than a mere gimmick, in that it allows full engine run up prior to take-off and dramatically shortens landing runs.

Droop nose This must surely be the ultimate in optional exotica, but it is the first thing spectators want to know about when you bring your 14-foot Concorde to the club field (Fig. 6.16).

Fig. 6.16. Droop nose down and the threshold coming up. Chris Golds' Concorde about to touch down in immaculate style at Abingdon.

7 OPERATION

This chapter covers pre-flight testing and checks, starting techniques, flying and maintenance.

A practice that I can thoroughly recommend is the keeping of a flight log. My flight log is really a diary in which I record not only every flight but also the modifications, maintenance work and failure diagnoses that I carry out. This has enabled me to analyse 300 ducted fan flights, noting every occasion when I was forced to cease flying for the day so that something could be put right back in the workshop or, in the case of write-offs, a dignified cremation could be arranged (Table 7.1).

In some cases, there has been more than one cause of damage. For example, if the engine fails on take-off and the pilot attempts an unsuccessful turn rather than land straight ahead, I have allocated ½ the fault to the engine and the other ½ to the pilot (usually me). I should also explain that some of the faults are interactive. For instance, if the basic design is not sound, this will increase the likelihood of construction faults and pilot errors.

Despite these provisos, certain messages are clear from Table 7.1. Firstly, design and construction faults taken together account for about a third of the failures. In principle, most of the problem areas have been covered in previous chapters but a few further points are worth making. Certain designs are more reliable than others. On one of my aircraft, I am lucky if I can get more than two flights without a failure whereas on another I can get 20 flights. True, the prime causes of failure are not necessarily attributed to the design as such, but consider for a moment a model that is prone to tip stalling because the designer (or builder) has omitted to provide adequate wash-out. Such a model will not tolerate the slightest error during a landing approach, whereas one with a properly designed wing will virtually land itself. If the designer does not get the undercarriage location or caster angles

Table 7.1

CAUSE	No. OF FAILURES	CRASHES (WRITE-OFFS)
Pilot error	20½	1
Engine and fuel supply	17½	3
Tuned pipe and fixings	12½	
Radio	2	1
Fan	3	
Design of model	15	1
Construction and assembly	13½	1
TOTALS	84	7

Showing numbers of failures and crashes attributable to various causes during a total of 300 ducted fan flights. A 'failure' was judged to be any problem with the aircraft that required a visit to the workshop to fix it (forcing abandonment of flying for the day).

right, there is a high likelihood of damage even before the aircraft leaves the ground.

The only write-off due to a construction fault was due to stupidity or vanity when I sanded almost through the glass cloth reinforcement at a wing root just to get a good finish. The inevitable result was the wing folding at the bottom of a Cuban-eight! Other construction faults have been due to things coming undone or unstuck. It is a long list and not one that I am proud of, as virtually all those faults could have been avoided by better workmanship or better inspection and testing, which is the subject of the next section.

7.1 Preflight inspection and testing

Let us assume that the aircraft is fully assembled and ready to go. It should not be necessary to say that the radio should be properly range-checked, with and without the engine running. If all is not well, with the transmitter forty yards away and the aerial down, don't fly until any faults have been corrected. Check that all surfaces move in the right direction and by the amount recommended by the designer. Check that you are fully familiar with all trims and mixing switches *without* having to look at the transmitter.

Fig. 7.1. SLEC propeller balancer modified to suit ducted fan impellers.

Table 7.1 suggests that radios are very reliable, having been responsible for only two failures, *but* one of those failures caused the aircraft to crash irreparably. Diagnosis of the cause of the crash revealed that one of the four battery cells had developed a high internal resistance. This only showed up as a problem when the battery was heavily loaded with all 5 servos moving at once. The battery voltage dropped below the critical level and the receiver ceased to function properly. It is probably justifiable to use a new receiver battery for the first flight of a precious new model.

All servo mounts and linkages should be checked by gripping flying surfaces to simulate flight loads, operating the radio, and observing the weak link (servo or linkage). If not satisfied, particularly with the primary controls (elevator and aileron), either change the servo or improve the linkage.

Like radios, fan units are remarkably reliable: only three failures and no write-offs. Make sure that the impeller is on tight, and that the fan unit will not dismantle itself during the flight. Check that the fan blades are free from surface damage and that there is nothing loose, or anything that could become loose, that might enter the fan during operation. This is not a problem with fully ducted inlets, of course.

Impeller manufacturing quality control has improved so much that it is not always necessary to balance the impeller before the first engine run-up. If the manufacturer's instruction book does call for the fan to be balanced, there are a number of commercial balancing jigs available such as the Sullivan Hi-Point balancer (USA) and the SLEC balancer (UK). The latter needs minor modification (Fig. 7.1) before it can be used for most impellers. Otherwise a simple home-made balancer will suffice (Fig. 7.2). Balance is best achieved by adding

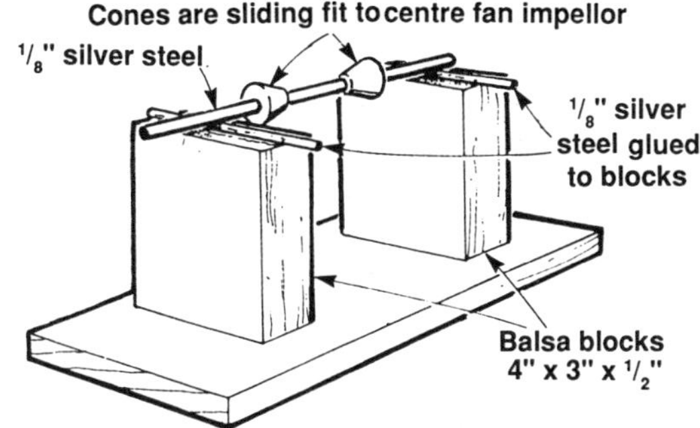

Fig. 7.2. Simple home-made fan balancer. Ensure that the two silver steel rods are parallel and horizontal by using a spirit level before gluing.

lead shot under the outer rim of the hub and securing with a suitable adhesive. Grinding off the heavy side should only be attempted if you are sure the structure will not be weakened.

It is easy to get quite neurotic about fan balancing: vibration can never be entirely eliminated from a piece of reciprocating machinery such as a two-stroke engine so you should not worry unduly about the fan.

Let us now take a look at the engine. Table 7.1 shows that the engine and tuned pipe system accounted for no less than 36% of all failures and 3 out of 7 write-offs, so this is an area where we really need to pay attention. Engine failure is almost always to do with the fuel supply. True, crankshafts do fail and plugs blow, but mechanical failures of that sort are quite rare. Having said that, some engines are much more tolerant to variations in the fuel supply. Furthermore, an old engine that is beginning to wear will be far less tolerant than a new engine. A sure sign that an engine needs some maintenance work is that it is beginning to be increasingly finicky about the needle valve setting.

Section 6.1 dealt fully with the fuel supply system but two final simple tests are worth doing. Remove the pressure line from the tuned pipe and pinch off the fuel supply line where it is connected to the carburettor. The tank filling tube should also be sealed. Blow through the pressure line and seal it off by pinching it for ten seconds. Release finger pressure and listen for escaping air. If nothing is heard, the system is leaking. Eliminate all leaks before proceeding further. Now fill the fuel tank(s) and disconnect the fuel supply line to the carburettor. Blow down the pressure line from the tuned pipe. Fuel should spurt from the carburettor line. If it merely trickles, something is wrong. Check for kinks in the tubes, debris in filters, tubes that are too small in diameter etc.

There is little to check on the engine itself other than the tightness

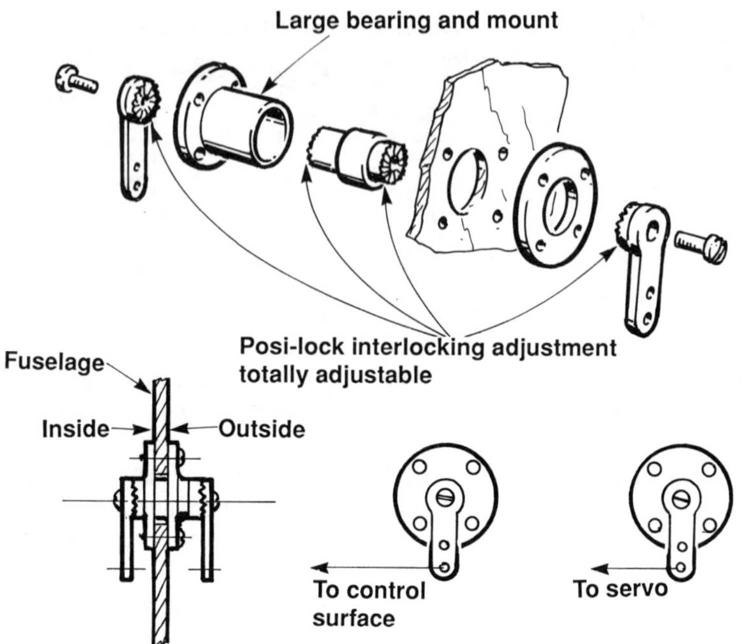

Fig. 7.3. The Robart feedthrough bellcrank is an excellent device for linking the throttle servo, which is outside the duct, to the carburettor throttle lever arm, which is inside the duct.

of cylinder head bolts, mounting bolts etc. Check the tuned pipe mounts and measure the critical length once more. Make sure that the throttle linkage does not bind or is likely to come detached. There are many ways of arranging the throttle linkage but probably the neatest is via a Robart feedthrough bellcrank (Fig. 7.3). This is infinitely adjustable and provides an excellent duct seal. It is also easy to dismantle when fan and engine are removed from the airframe. The throttle stop screw should be set so that the engine can be stopped by moving the throttle trim on the transmitter.

Now examine the airframe, starting with the control surfaces. Give them a sharp tug. Are the hinges secure? Are all clevises secured by short lengths of fuel tube so that they cannot open? Check the C.G. once again using a jig similar to that shown in Fig. 5.8. Set the aircraft on a flat base and check its attitude, rigging angles and washout. Check the load on the tail required to cause rotation and refer back to Section 5.8 to see whether the undercarriage needs to be moved. Check the functioning of the retracts if fitted. Push the aircraft along the ground and see that it tracks properly.

7.2 Starting techniques and engine tests

It will be assumed that the engine has been thoroughly run-in according to the manufacturer's instructions but that this will be its first operation in a ducted fan aircraft.

First, make sure that you have an assistant. He or she can help by steadying the aircraft, passing the transmitter etc. but, most of all, if things start to go wrong and an extra pair of hands is needed. I well remember dropping the glowplug connector and watching it demolish an entire impeller while the engine pitch increased to a crescendo until the hub 'exploded'! Owner and assistant should be equipped with ear defenders and safety glasses.

Several starting techniques are shown in Fig. 7.4. Not shown is the knotted string technique of the early pioneers, or the back flip of the pylon racers finger. The first is no longer needed and the second is to be avoided at all costs. With some installations it may be possible to insert a normal electric starter into the fuselage and engage the spinner as with a propeller-driven aircraft. Fig. 7.4(a) shows a simple modification that can be made to a starter which will allow access to

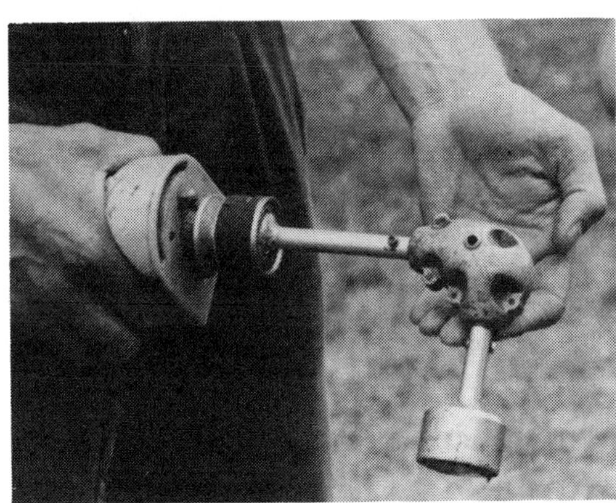

Fig. 7.4. Various starting devices. (a) Right angle drive attachment to conventional electric starter.

(b) Belt starting a TURBAX fan.

(c) Use of an extension shaft to start a BYROJET fan.

(d) Bob Violett starting his Sportshark with a VIOJETT starter extension.

a confined space. Otherwise a belt starter can be used, provided the spinner is fitted with a belt groove, Fig. 7.4 (b). Suitable belts are made for the model car fraternity. Alternatively 'V' type or toothed belts made for washing machines, or even full-size automobiles, may be adapted to ducted fan use. It is very easy to use a belt and I have never known one get caught in the fan.

Alternatively, starter extensions will have to be used. Byron Originals supply a rather sophisticated unit fitted with a free-wheeling device that comes into operation as soon as the engine has started, Figs. 7.4 (c) and 7.5 (a). I have never found any difficulty in starting the Byrojet fan by a simple modification to a normal starter, which involves making a 2 foot long ⅝ inch diameter aluminium extension shaft that is interposed between the electric motor and the aluminium cup that holds the rubber cone. The extension for the Viojett ducted fan unit (Fig. 7.4 [d] and 7.5 [b]) is a separate shaft that rotates in a brass sleeve that can be gripped with one hand. At one end, there is an aluminium spinner that is engaged by the electric starter in the

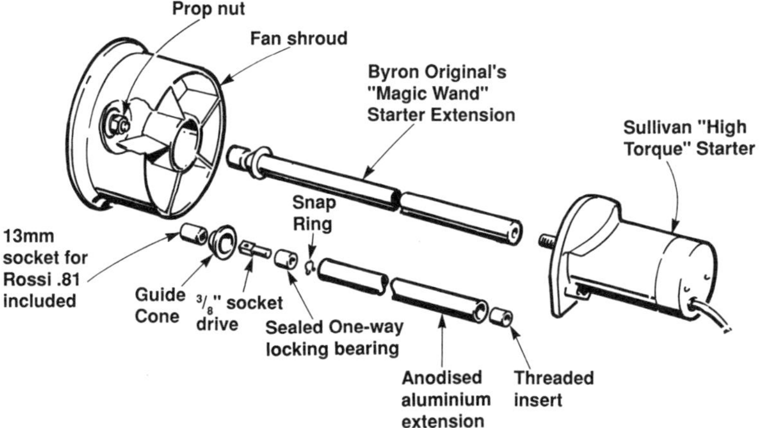

Fig. 7.5. Starter extensions. (a) Magic Wand system supplied by Byron Originals.

(b) Extension for VIOJETT fan.

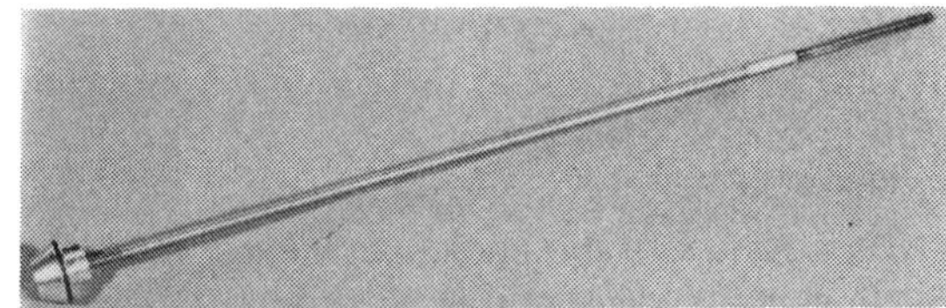

normal way and, at the other end, there is an Allen type ball-driver that engages the socket head cap screw securing the fan.

There are several ways to prime the engine. The carburettor is often inaccessible, so the fuel is usually forced into the carburettor by pressurizing the fuel tank. This can be done either by blowing down the pressure line or by placing a finger over the tuned pipe outlet while the engine is being cranked. With rear induction engines, the fuel can drain out of the carburettor rather than enter the crankcase unless the aircraft is tilted slightly. For installations that are prone to flooding, it is advisable to have a spring clip that can cut off the fuel flow to the carburettor until the engine is running properly.

Provided the fuel mixture is within a reasonable range, and the glow plug is glowing well, the engine should start very quickly. If the starter will not turn the engine over, it is either because it is flooded or the piston and sleeve are virtually stuck together with fuel oil residue from a previous run. Remove the plug and turn the engine over, injecting fuel into the cylinder head if necessary. When the engine is turning over freely with the starter, replace the glow plug and try again.

When the engine has started, gradually advance the throttle and lean out the mixture as necessary to reach full rpm. If a white band is painted diametrically across the spinner, an optical tachometer can be used to measure rpm. As soon as maximum speed has been reached, check the rpm and enrich the mixture slightly so that the rpm drops by 300 to 500 rpm. The exhaust should be visibly smoky at this point — make sure it always remains smoky throughout the entire flight. Now reduce the throttle and check for a reliable idle at, or below, 4000 rpm. Advance the throttle and make sure that the engine responds. If it doesn't, it may be because the idle mixture or mid-range mixture needs adjusting (if the carburettor is capable of such adjustment). If the engine still fails to transition properly, work your way through the following possibilities:

1) If the engine transitions better with the glow plug still connected to the power supply, try using a hotter plug.

2) Try a fuel with more nitromethane.

3) Try increasing the compression ratio by removing a cylinder head gasket or, better, using a different cylinder head insert.

4) Check that the fuel is not cavitating (bubbles in the tube to the carburettor).

5) Try restricting the tuned pipe outlet.

Supposing that the engine now idles and transitions satisfactorily, re-check the maximum rpm and compare with expectations from the manufacturer's literature on the engine and fan. If the rpm is down significantly on specification, check that the carburettor barrel is fully open at full throttle on the transmitter. It may be that the pipe length needs adjusting but proceed with care, especially if you have to cut the pipe or header. Another factor that can limit top end performance is the fan itself. Check that vibration levels are reasonable and that the blades are not rubbing. Finally, try a hotter plug or a fuel with higher nitromethane. If the problem still persists, the engine should be returned to the manufacturer.

Certain engines are capable of being re-worked to produce significantly higher power. The Rossi 81, for instance, can yield an extra 2000 rpm by increasing the exhaust port timing, inlet timing, and contouring of gas passages. All this is work that should be left to the expert. The K + B 7.5 9100 engine will produce significantly more power with a larger carburettor such as the OS7D. In both cases the engine will become more thirsty, so make sure the fuel supply can cope. The tuned pipe will also need to be adjusted.

It is now time to check the thrust. The simplest method is to attach a spring balance to the tail of the aircraft. There are, however, a few precautions to observe. The aircraft should be on a smooth, flat surface well away from impediments such as flight boxes, human legs, walls etc. that might obstruct airflow to the aircraft intakes. It is surprising what a difference this can make. I always record higher thrusts at the airfield compared with my garage. Secondly, the spring should be connected to the aircraft by a long string (about 6 feet) attached at a point roughly coincident with the thrust line. Note the spring balance reading as the aircraft is gently pulled backwards to overcome ground friction. Check the thrust in two directions (up and down wind). Average the values and note the rpm and atmospheric conditions (pressure, temperature and humidity). This will serve as a datum against which future performance can be compared. If the fan and duct arrangement does not change, there should be no need to measure thrust again provided the rpm can be measured. Remember Equation (8):

$$\text{Thrust} = (\text{rpm})^2 \times \text{constant}$$

as discussed in Chapter 2. Suppose you recorded 7 pounds of thrust at 22,000 rpm then the constant for your fan and ducting is:

$$\text{constant} = \frac{\text{Thrust}}{(\text{rpm})^2} = \frac{7}{(22,000)^2}$$

$$= 1.45 \times 10^{-8}$$

If you should change the fan in any way, or the ducts or inlets, this constant will need to be recalculated from new thrust measurements. Atmospheric changes can give rise to variations of $\pm 10\%$ in thrust.

There are better ways to measure thrust. Bob Kress advocates a pendulum arrangement which is free of friction and remarkably sensitive. It can accommodate anything from a fan in a stand to a fully assembled model aircraft (Fig. 7.6). Thrust, T, is determined by measuring the deflection of the pendulum at full thrust, (D inches) and calculating

$$T = \frac{WD}{L}$$

where L (inches) is the length of the wire supports and W is the total weight of the pendulum including the fan or aircraft. If W is given in pounds then thrust, T, will be calculated in pounds.

An alternative approach is to build a thrust stand or table like Barry Conway (Fig. 7.7). The platform, on which the fan or aircraft stands, rolls on small ball races to minimize friction. Thrust is measured by a spring balance. The beauty of Barry's stand is that it can be taken anywhere and will fit almost any aircraft by simply placing the main wheels in the aluminium channel. The only precaution to take is to ensure that the thrustline is roughly parallel to the direction of motion

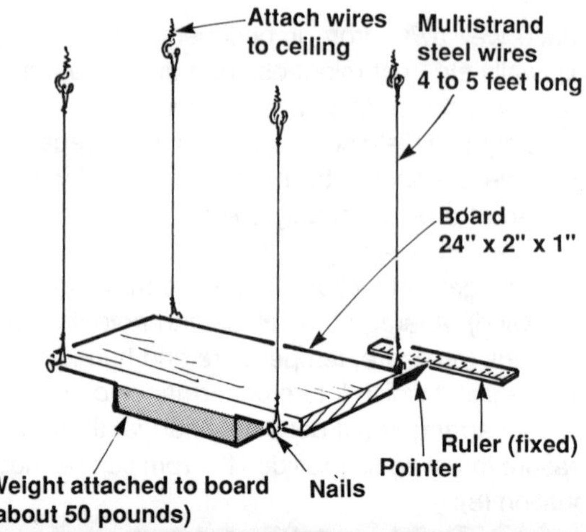

Fig. 7.6. Bob Kress's thrust pendulum.

of the platform. Yet another method I have seen used is to push a hand held pitot tube into the tailpipe. This will indicate dynamic pressure but it can be easily calibrated to read thrust in pounds. Subsequent measurements with the pitot then give a quick and easy indication of thrust for that aircraft.

The actual value of thrust measured at full rpm should be compared with the figure quoted by the aircraft designer. If no reference figure is available, you should not attempt a flight unless the thrust exceeds half the weight of the aircraft (a thrust-to-weight ratio of 0.5). If the measured T/W refuses to exceed 0.5 despite all your efforts, you may still manage a reasonable flight performance provided that you can get the aircraft into the air. After all, Fig. 5.33 shows that a model jet can maintain height with a T/W = 0.1. The next section will deal with various ways of getting the model airborne but, for the moment, draw comfort from the fact that many full size aircraft will fly very successfully with T/W ratios as small as 0.25 (Table 7.2).

Fig. 7.7. Barry Conway's thrust stand shown with Barry testing his F-104 Starfighter fitted with a VIOJETT.

7.3 Flying

Having completed the engine and fan tests, carefully re-examine the complete structure, as described in Section 7.1, to make sure that nothing has loosened, fallen off, or deteriorated significantly. If the fan has rubbed, remove the impeller and balance it. Before refitting it, gently relieve with abrasive paper that part of the shroud that was rubbed.

There are various ways of getting the model airborne:

1) Hand launch This should only be attempted for models with a low wing loading (less than 25 ounces per square foot) and a minimum T/W ratio of 0.7. If the wing loading is high, the stalling speed will also be high and you may not be able to exceed this speed before the aircraft hits the ground, unless there is a stiff head wind. Always launch the model slightly nose down.

2) Catapult or bungee launch This is not for the faint-hearted but I have seen it used very successfully both from the hand and from the

TABLE 7.2 THRUST TO WEIGHT (T/W) RATIOS FOR FULL SIZE AIRCRAFT

AIRCRAFT	ENGINE	STATIC THRUST (lb) T	WEIGHT (lb) W	T/W
VAMPIRE FB5	D. H. Goblin	3,350	11,000 loaded	0.30
SABRE F-86F	G. E. J47	5,800	13,200 combat	0.44
MiG-15	Nene type	6,000	11,300 combat	0.53
HUNTER 9	RR Avon	10,100	18,000 combat	0.56
LANSEN 32	RR Avon	11,000	16,500 combat	0.67
FOXBAT MiG-25	2 x Tumansky	35,000 dry	50,000 combat	0.70
		48,000 reheat	44,000 min.	1.10
EAGLE F-15	2 x P. and W.	50,000 reheat	26,000 min.	1.92
CONCORDE	4 x Olympus	152,000	400,000 full	0.38
BOEING 747	4 x PWJT9	190,000	775,000 full	0.25

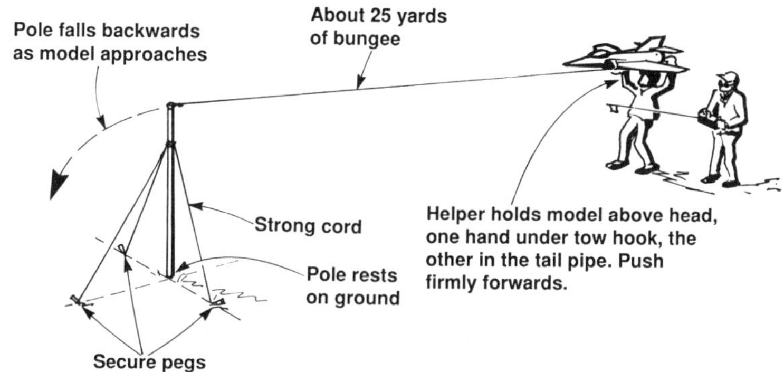

Fig. 7.8 Catapult launch system used by Peter and Paul Thorpe.

ground. The Thorpes perfected the first method using the arrangement shown in Fig. 7.8. The tow hook should be positioned just in front of the C.G. The second method is very similar but the aircraft is placed on the ground either on a dolly or its own undercarriage. The other end of the bungee is firmly pegged into the ground.

3) Dolly The most important consideration is for the horns (Fig. 5.18 [a]) to be just long enough to prevent premature lift off, but not so long that they hang on to the aircraft after it is airborne. They can be quite short if taking off from tarmac, but may need to be 2 or 3 inches long if using a bumpy grass surface. If the dolly does not have a separate servo-driven steerable nose leg, some care must be taken so that it tracks straight. As soon as ground speed builds up, the rudder should begin to take effect. Whatever happens, do not attempt to steer with the aileron control.

4) Fixed or retractable undercarriage These arrangements allow the luxury of extensive taxiing trials while the pilot plucks up courage for the big moment.

Make sure that the aircraft tracks properly and correct the nose wheel steering linkage as necessary. Make sure that both the nosewheel and rudder are neutral when the transmitter stick is at its neutral position with the trim centred. Generally speaking, aircraft with the main wheels set well out from the body and some castering action on the nose wheel are a delight to handle on the ground. Aircraft with narrow wheel bases and a nose leg that is angled forward are much more tricky. A little toe-in on the main wheels will help.

After taxiing trials, check out everything once more before refuelling and preparing for that first flight.

It is best to choose a day with a little head wind (no more than 15 mph) almost straight down the runway. If the wind is across the runway make sure that there is at least 300 feet available before the decision to abort has to be taken; that should leave ample room for the aircraft to slow down and turn before running into 'the rough'. Make sure you have a helper who is familiar with the trims on your transmitter just in case you cannot find them while piloting. Have him hold the aircraft pointing into wind while you check all controls for the last time. Run the engine to full throttle and hold it until any excess fuel has cleared. Signal your helper to release the model. Let it accelerate until you are sure it has achieved flying speed, then pull back on the elevator. Release any rudder you may have been holding, and prepare to shut the throttle if it hasn't lifted off by the time it reaches the abort point.

As soon as the model is airborne, try to keep the nose down, with a very shallow climb angle, while the aircraft continues to accelerate. It can take quite a long time before a ducted fan reaches full speed in level flight; perhaps 10 to 15 seconds in which time it could have travelled 2000 feet or more. It should, of course, be capable of turning well before top speed is reached, but pull it round gently in a wide circle before easing back on the power and trimming ailerons and elevator. Do a few left and right-hand circuits then gain some height and gradually reduce the throttle to explore its low speed handling. Try a gentle stall; recovery should be quick, as the C.G. should be well forward with most of the fuel still in the tank(s). This assumes that, as with almost all ducted fan models, the fuel is in front of the C.G. If the stall showed any vicious characteristics prepare for a landing, other-wise slowly advance the throttle to full power and put the plane into a prolonged steep climb. If the engine sags, it is probably too rich — look for the smoke trail. Next, put the plane in level flight and suddenly close the throttle to idle. If there is an abrupt change in attitude (nose up or down) the thrustline will need to be adjusted by changing the tailpipe angle. Roll inverted; if excessive down trim is required to maintain level flight, the C.G. is too far forward.

Slow the plane down again at a safe height and check the flaps. Note any change in pitch and correct with elevator trim. If the aircraft starts to roll when flaps are deployed this is a dangerous sign indicating that one flap is more effective than the other. Make a mental note of the roll direction so that it can be corrected after the plane has landed; in the meantime cancel the flaps and do not attempt to use them on landing. Open the throttle a little more abruptly and note the response of the aircraft. Ducted fan models are more sluggish in this respect than their propeller-driven counterparts. You probably also noticed that elevator response was less crisp at low speed. This is due to the lack of prop wash over the control surface.

All of these tests are designed to give some indication of how the model will behave during landing and, if the landing is aborted, how it will respond to the throttle when attempting a further circuit.

When preparing to land, execute a full rectangular circuit. The first (up-wind) leg should overfly the landing strip. Lower the undercarriage as the plane passes in front of you so that you can be sure all is well and you have 'three-greens'. After making a gentle turn, reduce the throttle on the down-wind leg. Make sure that there is plenty of speed before the final down-wind turns are attempted (this is specially important in the event of a dead stick landing). As soon as the aircraft is lined up with the runway, reduce the throttle to a safe idle. Most model jets are so clean aerodynamically that they will float a long way when straight and level. It is only during tight turns that a lot of speed and height can be lost (especially with deltas). Don't be too eager to put her down, otherwise an embarrassing and expensive bounce could result. Gently raise the nose without increasing height so that airspeed bleeds off until the aircraft can be flared out onto its mains (Fig. 7.9). It is surprising how slowly a swept wing or delta model can be flying at the point of touch-down. This is quite safe, provided the plane is properly designed and built and no attempt is made to turn it at the last moment.

Some very fast, clean models that do not possess flaps or airbrakes may require two full circuits before they can be slowed down sufficiently for landing.

Belly landings for models that take-off from a dolly are best attempt-

Fig. 7.9. A good landing begins with a good approach. Wings level with the nose coming up as the speed decays, in readiness for a perfect touchdown on the main wheels.

ed on short grass. Long grass has a tendency to pull the nose of the model down when contact is made. Landing speeds should be a little higher than for models with undercarriages so that the aircraft's attitude is closer to horizontal at the moment of touch-down. The belly of the aircraft is usually strengthened on such models. Belly protuberances, such as pitots, blisters, guns etc, should obviously be avoided. The landings should be dead stick to avoid ingestion of debris into the fan and engine.

Let us now turn back a page and consider the possible reasons for a failure to take-off. The causes are either a lack of elevator authority or inadequate ground speed or a combination of the two. The former has already been discussed in some detail. Solutions are: increase tailplane/elevator area, increase elevator throw, decrease tailplane load by moving the main wheels forward, or increase length of nose leg so that aircraft can fly-off rather than rotate, give the tailplane some negative camber.

Another way of looking at the second cause (lack of ground speed) is to consider the take-off distance. If your runway is of limited length, maybe the plane does not accelerate sufficiently rapidly for take-off speed to be reached before the plane runs out of runway. Take-off distance, d, can be estimated quite easily from the following equation:

$$d = \frac{0.033 \cdot V^2}{\dfrac{(T-D)}{W} - f} \tag{12}$$

where d is measured in feet, V is take-off speed in feet per sec. T (thrust), D (drag) and W (aircraft weight including fuel) are all measured in the same units (pounds in this case) and f is the coefficient of friction between the aircraft and the ground. The first thing to notice in equation (12) is that take-off distance, d, is smallest when the bottom line $\frac{(T-D)}{W} - f$ is largest.

This means that the coefficient of friction, f, should be as low as possible. With hard tyres on smooth tarmac, f could be as low as 0.05, whereas f could reach 0.3 for a grass field. Thrust and drag can be estimated from curves of the form shown in Fig. 5.33 which were produced for a particular high performance aircraft. Above 25 mph T-D decreases rapidly; at 88 mph T-D = 2.34 which gives $\left(\frac{T-D}{W}\right)$ = 0.3 for a plane weighing 7.8 pounds. This speed could never be reached on grass because $\left(\frac{T-D}{W}\right)$ -f = 0 thus the take-off run would have to be infinitely long, unless the take-off speed, V, could be reduced. Take-off speed must, of course, be greater than the stalling speed of the aircraft. Stalling speed, V_S, can be estimated from the following equation

$$V_S = 7.3 \sqrt{\frac{w}{C_L}} \qquad (13)$$

where w is the wing loading in ounces/square foot and C_L is the lift coefficient of the wing at the point of stall. For the aircraft described in Fig. 5.33, w = 7.8 x 16 x 144/640 = 28 ounces/square foot and C_L = 1.2 (without flaps). This gives a stalling speed V_S = 35 feet/sec. A safe take-off speed would therefore be, say, 44 feet/sec (or 30 mph). If we substitute this value in equation (12) and read off T-D = 6.1 from Fig 5.33, we can calculate take-off distance.

d = 132 feet for a grass field

or   d = 87 feet for smooth tarmac.

To summarize, take-off distance can be minimized by: reducing ground friction, increasing thrust, reducing drag, reducing weight, reducing wing loading and increasing the lift coefficient (try using flaps for take-off). Catapult assist can also help, as can a strong head wind. A cheat intake through the wing can make matters worse, in that the wing becomes less efficient as a lifting device. This is equivalent to a reduction in C_L which means a higher stalling (and take-off) speed. On the other hand, the static thrust may be improved by judiciously introducing cheat intakes at other locations, such as the fuselage, so that C_L is not affected.

After the first flight, adjust the control surfaces to neutralize the transmitter trim positions and make such other corrections as may be necessary. Check the structure of the aircraft and fan thoroughly, using the same check list as detailed at the beginning of this Section. Bob Violett used to virtually strip down his A-4 Skyhawk in between competition flights.

Subsequent flights should be much more relaxed, enabling a full exploration of the flight envelope to be made. If you timed the first flight and noted how much fuel was left in the tank(s), this will give a good indication as to how long you can safely fly. Try not to fly at full throttle all the time. It should only be necessary for take-off and vertical manoeuvres. Sensible throttle usage is not only more scale-like but it extends flight times and engine life.

Table 7.1 showed that pilot error was one of the most common causes of 'failure' for my aircraft. This obviously depends upon pilot competence but there are a few pointers that might help:

1) Do not fly when weather conditions are not suitable.

2) Always try to have sufficient height and speed so that, in the event of engine failure, a proper landing pattern can be established.
3) Time flights so that the chance of an unplanned dead-stick landing is minimized.
4) If anything sounds wrong (engine noise change or flutter) or feels wrong (unexplained change of trim or instability), reduce throttle and land immediately.
5) Avoid too-tight turns that lose speed, especially at low altitude. Keep manoeuvres wide and smooth.
6) Avoid taking off with insufficient airspeed and landing too fast or too far away.
7) Resist the temptation to enter club competitions (spot landings, limbos etc.!)

8 KITS AND PLANS

The number of manufacturers producing a range of ducted fan kits (more than one or two basic designs) can be counted on the fingers of one hand and, of these, only two have been in the business for more than three years. There are, on the other hand, many one or two-kit manufacturers, but most of these work on a 'cottage industry' basis. The situation is very fluid with kits becoming available for a while and then disappearing from the scene with startling rapidity. This makes a review of ducted fan kits and plans little more than a 'snapshot in time'. The reader should, therefore, be aware that the following list will be out of date by the time he reads it, although every attempt has been made to ensure that the products listed are generally available at the time of going to press. For readers requiring more details, many of the kits and plans have been reviewed in the modelling press and are referred to in Appendix 2.

8.1 Kits

This section is dealt with in alphabetical order by country and manufacturer. Addresses are given in Appendix 1.

Belgium — Philip Avonds Scale Jets Philip shot to fame with his splendid first place in the 1988 World Scale Championships with his *F-15 Eagle* (Fig. 8.1). The semi-kit consists of all the fibreglass work, vacuum formings, decals, foam core wings and special mechanisms, and builds into a 1:9 scale model weighing 16-17 pounds, length 85 inches and is suited to two .45 size fans and engines.

Canada — Bob Parkinson Flying Models This company specializes in semi-scale jets of simple built-up construction. Their original kit of the *Avro Arrow CF 1000 Delta* was followed by the *Regal Eagle*. This

Fig. 8.1. F-15 Eagle by Philip Avond's Scale Jets. Won World Scale Championship at Gorizia, Italy 1988.

Fig. 8.2. 'Blue Hornet' from Bob Parkinson Flying Models fitted here with a GLEICHAUF fan and PICCO-80 engine, it was originally designed to use a BYROJET.

design is based on the *F-15 Eagle* but uses a single Byrojet fan and has a cheat inlet in the belly. Weight is 8 pounds, length 65 inches.

Bob followed the Eagle with another promising kit based on the F-18 Hornet. He calls this the *Blue Hornet* (Fig. 8.2). It is also based on the Byrojet Fan Unit and weighs 9 pounds, length 63 inches. Most of these kits can, of course, be modified to suit.

Canada — Yellow Aircraft and Hobby Supplies Ltd Dr. Jack Tse's team of enthusiastic ducted fan model designers, builders and flyers have had many notable successes to their credit, the most remarkable being the large twin fan, swing-wing *F-14 Tomcat* (Fig. 1.13). His new company's ambitious plan is to have no less than ten ducted fan kits available to the public including big twins like the *F-14, F-15, F-18* and *SR-71 Blackbird.* Several prototypes of the *F-18 Hornet* have been built, including the one in Fig. 8.3, by Bob Fiorenze. Single fan projects include the *T-38, F-16, F-20* and *Mirage.* So far the only kits to be advertised are the *A-4 Skyhawk* (weight 9 pounds, length 56 inches), the *SR-71 Blackbird* (weight 20 pounds, length 105 inches)

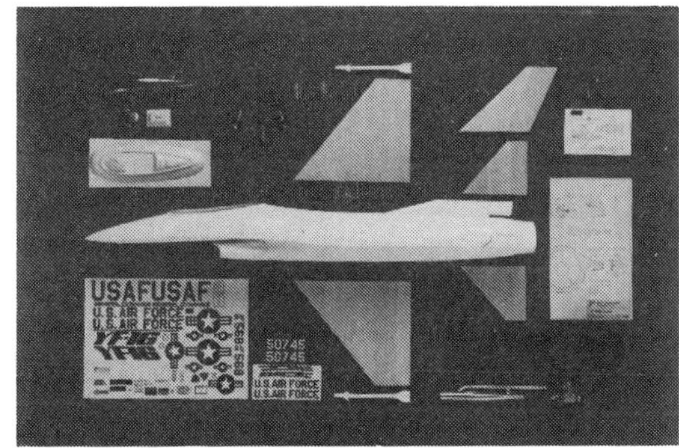

the *F-5E Freedom Fighter* (weight 8¾ pounds, length 76 inches) and the *F-15 Eagle* (length 91 inches). Kits are based on conventional fibreglass moldings and may be purchased with fans and engines. Dr. Tse has tended to standardise on the OS-77/Dynamax power package.

Germany — Gleichauf Modellbautechnik Rolf Gleichauf's only ducted fan kit is a scale *F-16* based on his own fan unit, although it would also be ideally suited to a Byrojet. It weighs 11 pounds, length 73 Inches. It appears to be a conventional fibreglass and foam semi-kit, the purchaser being required to supply some wood, wheels, control rods, tanks etc. (Fig. 8.4).

Germany — HR-Modelltechnik (Bauer) This long-established company produces two kits both based on their own ducted fan units. The *Heinkel 162 Salamander* is an unusual early German jet with a 'V'-tail. The engine is mounted in a pod above the fuselage. It weighs 8 pounds, span 54 inches. The *Skyhawk* is a more conventional model, weight 11 pounds, length 70 inches.

Fig. 8.5. Alec Cornish-Trestrail's attractive version of the Kyosho Tommycat kit.

Fig. 8.6. John Carpenter's Folland Gnat.

Germany — Krick Modellbau Herr Krick's semi-scale *Folland Gnat* offers a low cost introduction to ducted fans, as it can utilize the Micromold fan unit and an inexpensive .45 size motor. Weight is just over 7 pounds, span 48 inches.

Japan —Kyosho The only ducted fan kit produced by this company was designed by Bob Kress. It is a character-scale kit of the F-14 which Bob calls the *Tommycat*. It is a small model based on the RK20B fan unit, weighs 4 pounds, span 33 inches and is of built-up construction (Fig. 8.5).

United Kingdom — John Carpenter Models John's semi-kit is of the *Folland Gnat* and is most often seen painted in its Red Arrow's livery. Designed around popular 45 size fans and engines, its all-up weight is 10-12 pounds (Fig. 8.6).

United Kingdom — Turbofan This company produces two approximately 1:8 scale semi-kits of the classic dogfighters from the Korean

Fig. 8.7. Three of Bob Violett's models. On the left his Aggressor and on the right the new Viper. The pretty one in the middle is daughter Patty holding a Sportshark.

War. The *F-86 Sabre* weighs 9 pounds, span 57 inches, and is suited to .40 to .65 fans and engines (Fig. 6.7). The *MiG-15* weighs 10 pounds, span 54 inches and can use either a Byrojet or a Viojett fan unit (engine size .65 to .90). Both kits feature glass fibre fuselages and foam wings.

USA — Air Flair Manufacturing Co. The only ducted fan kit produced by this small American Company is a scale twin *Me 262*, weight 17 pounds, span 84 inches. The semi-kit uses a glass fibre fuselage and built-up wings. The manufacturer recommends Dynamax fan units.

USA — Bob Diveley Model Aircraft Inc. The *BAe Hawk* manufactured by this company was one of the first ducted fan kits produced in the USA. It is suited to a .45 size fan unit and weighs 8½ pounds, span 54 inches. The kit features built-up construction throughout.

USA — Bob Violett Models Bob returned to the kit manufacturing business a few years ago when he retired from full-size aviation. He produces four kits, based on his Viojett Fan Unit. The kits are complete and feature sport type models designed for optimum performance. Fig. 8.7 shows his current stable. The two aircraft on the left are versions of his original *Sportshark* design (the *Aggressor* has a longer nose and F-5 type fin). The aircraft on the right is the swept wing *Viper*. Weighing 9½ pounds, span 50 inches, length 67 inches, its aerodynamic refinements yield speeds exceeding 170 mph. Bob's kits feature epoxy/glass fuselages and built-up wings, together with considerable use of carbon fibre to increase strength and reduce weight. A further refinement of the original *Sportshark* design is now available, designated *Aggressor II*. This kit features strengthened Kevlar doublers and Magnacore wings of thinner section giving top speeds well over 180 mph.

Bob Violett models have recently entered the scale scene with an

F-86F Sabre featuring the Viojett fan, scale inlets and outlets and scale working retracts.

USA — *Byron Originals* This Iowa-based company is the largest manufacturer of ducted fan kits in the world. They produce ten kits, of which the *MiG-15* and *F-16* have recently been re-vamped to introduce design and construction improvements that have been developed since they were first produced in 1979/80. All Byron kits are complete and are based on their Byrojet fan unit. They feature polyester glass fuselages, foam wings and many fascinating design innovations. Other Byron kits are the *A-4 Skyhawk, KFIR, F-86H* and *F-86D, F-20 Tigershark, BD-5J* and, quite recently, a sport model called the *Bullet*. Undoubtedly the flagship of this fleet is the *F-15 Eagle* twin fan model (Fig. 8.8). The aircraft weighs 28 pounds with a thrust capability of 24 pounds. It is 105 inches long and features a dorsal speed brake, pneumatic wheel brakes, and specially designed retracts. The latest release is a single fan *F-18 Hornet* (length 84 inches, weight 18 pounds).

USA — *Century Jet Models* Two semi-kits are available utilizing fibreglass fuselages and foam wings, suited to the Byrojet or Dynamax fans. The *Sport Hawk* weighs 10 pounds, length 59 inches, and the *F-100 Super Sabre* weighs 11.5 pounds, length 63 inches.

USA — *Cressline Model Products* These are relative newcomers to the ducted fan field manufacturing three complete scale kits. All feature fibreglass fuselages and built up wings. The *Saab Viggen* is 1:9 scale and weighs 10 pounds, length 64 inches. The *F-20 Tigershark* weighs 10 pounds, length 70 inches and the new *F-100 Super Sabre* weighs 10 pounds and is 67 inches long. The

Fig. 8.9. This team of enthusiastic Belgian modellers built the Tomcat from a JET AGE kit. The twin BYROJETS and ROSSI-90s give plenty of power for realistic flight.

manufacturer recommends the Dynamax fan for all three models.

USA — *Custom R/C Aircraft* Another recent entry into ducted fan kit manufacture, George Miller's company produces one kit of the *Phantom*. The model uses a single Byrojet fan mounted upright. Weight is around 10 to 11 pounds. His second kit, the *F-8 Crusader,* uses the same power plant, weighs 10 pounds, length 72 inches, and features blow-in doors with no inlet duct.

USA — *Hobby Barn* Whereas manufacturers may come and go, certain designs seem to go on forever. So it is with the Hobby Barn *F-86 Sabre* which was first attributed to Air Forms and later to Zia Models. The kit is now offered in comprehensive form. The finished model weighs 8-9 pounds, uses foam wings and fibreglass fuselage and spans 51 inches. It is suited to .45 to .65 size fans. This company also produces a *F-100 Super Sabre.*

USA — *Hyatt Tech* Little is known about this company other than it produces a good looking twin fan model of the *Learjet-35.*

USA — *Jet Age Model Aircraft Co.* Jet Age is noted for its range of fans which use scimitar-shaped blades. In 1986 it advertised a range of six kits including a number of large twins, like the *SR-71 Blackbird* which

Fig. 8.10. Jet Hangar Hobbies A-4 Skyhawk built by the author. Weight 9½ pounds with retracts, TURBAX I and K&B 7.5cc engine.

Fig. 8.11. Jet Model Products Starfire Sport model. Uses DYNAMAX fan and 0S-77 DF engine.

can also be fitted with a *D-21 Drone*. The 108-inch long fuselage is fibreglass and the kit is suited to two 45 size fans. Other twins include a *Lear Jet* for .81 engines, a swing-wing *F-14 Tomcat* (Fig. 8.9), a 1:2 scale *S-3A Viking*, and an *F-18 Hornet*. The only single fan model is a *F-104 Starfighter*.

USA — Jet Hangar Hobbies Larry Wolfe's company pioneered ducted fan kit production in the USA. All models are based on its two fan units — the Turbax I and Turbax III — and all are accurate scale kits, with the possible exception of the *F-86 Sabre* which was designed as a ducted fan trainer. The early products were semi-kits utilizing epoxy/glass fuselages and built-up wings. The *Mirage/KFIR, F9F-8 Cougar*, and *A-4 Skyhawk* (Fig. 8.10) were from this period. More recently, Larry has produced an *A-7 Corsair II* which features foam wings and special retracts. His latest release is a single fan 1:10 scale *Phantom*. Larry has produced a special tuned pipe with a split exhaust to go with this kit. The model is 68 inches long and weighs 10 pounds.

Fig. 8.12. Knights of the Air F-20 Tigershark (originally a World Engineering kit).

USA — Jet Model Products Tom Cook is probably best known for his large twin fan *Phantom* with which both he and Bob Fiorenze have competed successfully since 1980. The original kit used two Turbax I fans with K&B 7.5 engines, but now Tom recommends his own Dynamax fans with OS-77 engines. Tom's second kit is a sport model called the *Starfire* (Fig. 8.11). The kit is very comprehensive and has recently been updated (*Starfire II*) to include full flow fibreglass inlet ducts, separately molded access hatch, computer-designed airfoils etc.

USA — Knights of the Air World Engineering sold all manufacturing rights to their kits and plans to Knights of the Air, including the beautiful *Tigershark* shown in Fig. 8.12. The model uses a Byrojet, is 88 inches long and weighs 14 pounds. The 1:12 scale *Lockheed U-2 Spyplane* weighs 9 pounds, spans 80 inches for a .45 size fan. The twin-fan *MiG-25 Foxbat* has two BOSS 602 fans, weighs 16 pounds, length 73 inches. Finally, the *SR-71 Blackbird* weighs 20 pounds, length 108 inches.

USA — MDM The 56 inch long, 8.5 pound, *F-18 Hornet* is claimed to be an Almost Ready to Fly (ARF) kit requiring only 3 hours assembly work before finishing. It is suited to Turbax I or Dynamax fans (engine size .45 to .77). The company also produces the *F-18* and an *F-16* in kit form.

USA — Midwest Products Co. Inc. This company pioneered the development of simple kits for the smaller size fan units. Their *Jetster* was designed by Dick Sarpolus as a ducted fan trainer. The RK-20B fan is carried in a pod above the fuselage. Wingspan is 48 inches. The *A-4 Skyhawk* is based on the RK-049 fan. Designed for hand launching it weighs 25 ounces, with a span of 36 inches. Their largest model is the *Heinkel He-162* originally designed to use the Axiflo RK-40 fan. None of these fan units are currently available, but see Chapter 3 for suitable substitutes.

USA — Pauls Flying Staff Now produces the *F-86 Sabre* previously manufactured by House of Balsa. This very successful design was

Fig. 8.13. Thorpe Brothers Tigershark, shown here fitted with an effective, but inconspicuous, dolly.

originally intended for a .20 size fan unit, although it is now most frequently flown with the new RK-740 fan which gives a higher thrust-to-weight ratio.

USA — South East Model Products This company specialises in relatively small models designed by Nick Ziroli based on the company's own Aerojet 25 fan units. The *F-15 Eagle* weighs 5 pounds, length 51 inches, and the *F-4F Phantom* weighs 5 pounds, length 50 inches. Both kits are semi-scale, of fully built-up wooden construction and contain all necessary wood, hardware, wheels and canopies.

USA — Super Sonics This company is new to the ducted fan scene. Its first kit is a sport scale *A.7 Corsair* suited to the Turbax I fan unit, and weighs only 6 pounds, span 48 inches. The aircraft is of balsa and foam construction (no fibreglass). The second kit is a sport model called *The Predator.* Again of balsa and foam construction, it weighs 8.5 pounds span 54 inches and suits .45 to .77 engines.

Fig. 8.14. Trevor Waters' A-10 Thunderbolt complete with bomb-dropping option.

USA — Zack-o Plastics Most recent addition to the ranks of American ducted fan kit manufacturers Zack-o produce an all-wooden version of the *F-15 Eagle*. Length is 60 inches, weight 7 pounds. Based on the Dynamax fan, the kit can be ordered partially pre-built.

8.2 Plans

The best known producers of ducted fan model plans are the Thorpe Brothers. Their plans of the *F-18 Hornet, FGR2 Phantom, Delta-fighter, F-20 Tigershark* (Fig. 8.13), and *Mirage F-1C* are based on .45 size fan units of which their own Thorjet unit is typical. The plans are supplied with instructions, a duct sample and control cable and tubing. The designs are of wooden, built-up, construction. Bob Holman is marketing the Thorpe Brother's plans in the USA.

Nick Ziroli produces plans for wooden constructions of the *F-15 Eagle* and *A-4 Phantom* which are also sold in kit form by South East Model Products (see Section 8.1).

In Italy G. Bertella sells a range of plans suited to the Bauer fan units; canopies are also available. The following single engine models all weigh 7-8 pounds – *F-16, F84-F, F-86, F-100, F104, MiG-21, MiG-15* and *Mirage 2000*. The twin-engined models weigh 11-13 pounds – *SR-71, MRCA Tornado, F-14* and *F-15*.

Several magazine publishers run their own plans services. Most notable are the ASP Plans in the UK which include a *MiG-15* and *Grumman Panther* by Marcus Norman, a *BAe Hawk* by Paul Gray, an *A-10 Thunderbolt* by Trevor Waters (Fig. 8.14), a *Delta-1000* sport model by Graham Dennett, an *F-86 Sabre* by the Thorpe Brothers and a *Saab Viggen* by Alberto Ghisleri. ASP Plans Service also supply vacuum formed fittings such as canopies. Occasionally foam and veneered wings can also be provided.

In Germany, the publishers Verlag fur Technik und Handwerk (VTH) produce plans for the *Alpha Jet* by Heinrich Voss, the *Heinkel 612 Salamander* by Norbert Gallena, and the *Me 262* by S. Glockner.

In the United States, *Model Airplane News* sells plans for an *F-14 Tomcat* by Norman Gupton and an *F-84* by Walter Musciano.

Radio Control Modeller (USA) has plans by Marc Frankel for the *Vigilante,* and, very recently, a Learjet 35A for twin Dynamax fans, also by Art Johnson for the *F-100 Super Sabre* and the futuristic *Star Cobra*.

Flying Modeller (USA) publishes plans for Eric Baughers *Performance Phantom*.

Scale R/C Models (USA) has plans for Colonel Bob Thacker's *Saab Viggen* and *Phantom*, Bob Parkinson's *Avro Arrow* and George Miller's *A-10 Warthog*.

9 THE FUTURE

A quick look at the list of references or magazine articles on ducted fans at the end of this book indicates the growth of interest in this exciting facet of aeromodelling. Prior to 1980, there had been just a handful of articles by pioneers like the Normans, Scozzafarva and Kress but then, quite suddenly, things took off. Table 9.1 tells the story:

TABLE 9.1

Numbers of magazine articles and books about ducted fans collected by the author.

YEAR	NUMBER OF MAGAZINE ARTICLES
1955-1975	5
1976	2
1977	3
1978	4
1979	3
1980	21
1981	14
1982	22
1983	27
1984	22
1985	36
1986	53
1987	49
1988	53

Fig. 9.1. Ducted fan fly-ins continue to attract large numbers of fliers and spectators.

The list is not exhaustive but contains most of the articles published in English language magazines and a few in foreign languages.

The growth of interest coincided with the production of the first commercial fans and kits. During the past three years, there has been a second, dramatic, growth of interest. This is reflected, not only in the number of magazine articles, but in that other index of enthusiasm — the Fly-in.

The first Ducted Fan Fly-in was held at Abingdon in 1981 to commemorate the success of Sir Frank Whittle's jet engine. Since then, this event has become increasingly popular (Fig. 9.1) and in 1988 became really international with visitors from Sweden, Germany, France, Belgium, and Czechoslovakia. A total of 68 aircraft were registered for flying and at least two dozen more were on static display. This scene is repeated in many countries around the world. In 1988 in the USA there were at least eight Fly-ins including the Byron Aviation Expo and the Tangerine International Championships, both of which have separate sessions for ducted fans.

Despite this apparently healthy scene, there remains a nagging suspicion that relatively few new members are joining the movement. The faces at the Fly-ins and the names in the magazines do not seem to be changing very rapidly.

There have always been more 'watchers' than 'doers' in this area of specialism. This is partly due to the apparent complexity of the subject and the cost of the initial investment, although the latter impediment has not deterred large numbers of helicopter addicts. The reputation for unreliability of ducted fan models may have something to do with it. Watching a frustrated 'fan-addict' struggling for hours with a temperamental high-revving racing engine must have dissuaded a few potential converts, as has the spectacle of an underpowered 'lead sled' struggling to maintain altitude. Such drawbacks have all but disappeared, however, and we now have ducted fan aircraft that could give a pylon racer a run for its money. It isn't that ducted fan models are difficult to fly; anyone with experience of a low wing aerobatic machine should have no difficulty with a ducted fan aircraft, provided it is not underpowered or overweight.

Their spirit, I feel, is willing but something is undoubtedly holding back the potential avalanche of new recruits. Lack of suitable flying sites must be one factor. It is true that many scale jets are really best suited to hard-surfaced runways, but there are many other ducted fan models that perform well off grass. The key is to keep the thrust-to-weight ratio high and the wheels large. There is also room for the development of a range of smaller hand-launched models powered by some of the incredibly powerful .21 size engines developed for car racing.

The other big factor affecting flying site availability is the much more serious question of noise. There is no denying the fact that ducted fans are generally noisier than most prop-driven models. Moreover, the noise is of higher frequency and hence more irritating. Curiously, however, this difference is more noticeable while the aircraft are on the ground rather than when they are flying, in which case the ducted fan may actually be quieter due to the greater attenuation with distance of high frequency sounds. Nevertheless, something needs to be done and is receiving attention by manufacturers such as Bob Violett and Tom Cook who are experimenting with carbon fibre pipes. The approach I prefer is to use steel pipes (see Chapter 4) on the basis that there is no substitute for mass of material when it comes to isolating a source of noise. Whatever route is chosen, there will be a loss of power or an increase in weight, but that is a price we must pay.

Electric powered ducted fans would, of course, provide a total solution to the ducted fan problem. Several articles have been written on the subject but I have yet to see an electric powered jet fly, although success must be very close.

The other factor that may be deterring a large number of converts is the lack of well-proven ARTF (almost-ready-to-fly) kits. I am sure that this development is almost upon us and will certainly yield rich rewards to the first large manufacturer who succeeds.

There are relatively few specialist organisations serving the ducted fan modeller, but the situation is beginning to change. In Germany the Deutscher Modellflieger-Verband ev. (DMVF) features a section dedicated to the interests of ducted fan fliers. In the USA, Dave Tyson has formed a Jet Pilots Organisation (JPO) and in the UK, Alec Cornish-Trestrail produces a Newsletter for British enthusiasts. Detailed addresses are given in Appendix 1.

There are, on the other hand, almost too many ducted fan units on the market. As I write this chapter I am aware of the new VECTOR fan being produced in the USA and the RAM-AIR fan in the UK. The latter unit uses the MICROMOLD blades but is otherwise fabricated entirely from metal. It can be provided with 5, 6, 7 or 8 blades for .40 to .90 size engines. The limited market simply will not support such a profusion of products and some rationalization will surely take place. The same is true to a lesser extent with special ducted fan engines. At the end of the day, we modellers will benefit from the survival of the fittest but, in the meantime, selection of a suitable fan/engine combination will remain a confusing and risky business for the first-time fan buyer.

Turning now to the cutting edge of the new technology; there seems to be only one major challenge left to conquer — that of a true VTOL (Vertical Take-Off-and Landing) model of the Harrier. Many dedicated modellers have attempted this pinnacle and many have given up, but not so with Mike Koskela. Mike is now on his twentieth version of the Harrier and has achieved reliable vertical take-off, hover and landing but has not yet managed the transition to level flight and

Fig. 9.2. Two ways to solve the V.T.O. problem. (a) Mike Koskela's Harrier uses proportional flap valves, whereas

(b) Nick Astley-Cooper uses a vectored nozzle arrangement.

Fig. 9.3. What a team Mike Koskela and Gerry Jackman would make if they could combine their energies to put a real jet engine in a model Harrier!

back. The problems are severe. A thrust-to-weight ratio considerably in excess of 1:1 is required with a ducting system that is bound to give large efficiency losses. Added to that, there is the vectored thrust control problem and the need for heavy gyros to give stability. Fig. 9.2 (a) shows Mike's approach based on variable flap valves and Fig. 9.2 (b) shows a system of rotating nozzles favoured by RAF Engineer Nick Astley-Cooper. One can only wonder at the dedication and inventiveness of such people and offer them every encouragement.

Perhaps, one day, Mike Koskela will team up with Gerry Jackman, designer of the world's smallest gas turbine, to produce a successful VTOL Harrier (Fig. 9.3). A turbofan would be required, of course, with a high by-pass ratio, but individually Mike and Gerry have already solved so many problems that surely this would not beat them.

Apart from this one elusive goal there really are no limits to the type of jet aircraft we might wish to build. Models can be large or small, complex or simple, scale, aerobatic, fast or slow. We have the technology and it is up to us to use it to satisfy our creative needs, and for the pure spine-tingling thrill of model jet flight.

APPENDIX 1
MANUFACTURERS AND
SUPPLIERS ADDRESSES

Air Flair Manufacturing Co., P.O. Box 11702, Kansas City, Missouri 64138, USA.

Argus Specialist Publications Ltd., Plans Service, Argus House, Boundary Way, Hemel Hempstead, Hertfordshire, HP2 7ST, England.

G. Bertella, Via Matteotti, 248 Gardone V.T. 25063 (Brescia) Italy.

Bob Diveley Model Aircraft Inc., 28001 Chagrin Boulevard, Suite 206, Woodmere, Ohio 44122, USA.

Bob Parkinson Flying Models, 3 William Street, Thornton, Ontario, LOL 2NO, Canada.

Bob Violett Models, 1373 Citrus Road, Winter Springs, Florida 32708, USA.

Bob Holman Plans, P.O. Box 741, San Bernadino, Ca 92402, USA.

Byron Originals, P.O. Box 279, Ida Grove, Iowa 51445, USA.

Century Jet Models, P.O. Box 111, Rantoul, Il 61866, USA.

Chart-Micromold, Chart House, Station Road, East Preston, Littlehampton, W. Sussex, BN16 3AG, England.

Alec Cornish-Trestrail, 23 The Avenue, Charlton Kings, Cheltenham, Glos, GL53 9BL, England.

Cressline Model Products Inc., W.239N.1690 Busse Road, Waukesha, Wisconsin 53188, USA.

Custom R/C Aircraft, 249 Robin Way, Santa Rosa, California 95407, USA.

Deutscher Modellfliegen-Verband e.v. (Heinrich Voss) Im Mallingforst 50, 4250 Bottrop, W. Germany.

Force Air Technology Inc., 9275 Trade Place, Suite G, San Diego, California 92126, USA.

Flying Models, Carstens Publications Inc, Fredon-Springdale Road, Fredon Township, P.O. Box 700, Newton, New Jersey, 07860, USA.

Hobby Barn, East 21st Street, Tucson, Arizona 85733, USA.

HR-Modelltechnik, Haupstrasse 2, 8011 Forsten, West Germany.

Hyatt Tech, 45 Marchwood Road, Exton, Pa 19341, USA.

Jet Age Model Aircraft Co., 5428 Bushnell, Riverside, California 92505, USA.

Jet Hangar Hobbies 121308 Carson Street, Hawaiian Gardens, California 90716, USA.

Jet Pilots Organisation (Dave Tyson), 1200 Queen Elaine Drive, Casselberry, Fl 32707, USA.

Jet Model Products, 304 Silvertop Road, Raymore, Missouri 64083, USA.

K.B. Lyco, Box 5006, S-79105, Falun, Sweden.

Knights of the Air, 1400 Route 32, West Friendship, Maryland 21794, USA.

*K&B Manufacturing*12152 Woodruffe Avenue, Downey, California 90241, USA.

Kress Jets Inc., 4308 Ulster Landing Road, Saugerties, New York 12477, USA.

Krick Modellbau, Postfach 24, D-7134 Knittlingen/Wurtt, West Germany.

MDM, 9255 Survey Road No-12, Elk Grove, Ca 95624, USA.

Midwest Products Co. Inc., 400 South Indiana Street, Hobart, Indiana 46342, USA.

Model Airplane News, Air Age Inc, 632 Danbury Road, Wilton, Connecticut 06897, USA.

Nick Ziroli Models, 29 Edgar Drive, Smithtown, New York 11787, USA.

OPS, P.O. Box (Casella Postale) 129, 20052 Monza, Italy.

OS Engines Manufacturing Co. Ltd., 6-15 3-chome, Imagawa, Higashisumiyashi-ku, Osaka 546, Japan.

Paul's Flying Stuff, P.O. Box 121, Escondido, California 92025, USA.

Philip Avonds Scale Jets, Dorpstraart 18, B-8458 Koksijde, Belgium.

Picco Motors, Via C. Cattaneo 8, I-20052 Monza, Italy.

Radio Control Modeller, 120 West Sierra Madre Boulevard, Sierra Madre, California 91024, USA.

Ram-air, 117 Stopes Brow, Blackamoor Village, Blackburn, Lancashire BB3 0QP, England.

Rolf Gleichauf Modellbautechnik., Zeppelinstrasse 12, 7710 Donaneschingen, West Germany.

Rossi Electronica Bresciana s.r.1., Via Caporalino 5/7, 25060 Cellatica (Brescia) Italy.

Scale R/C Modeller, Challenge Publications, 7950 Deering Avenue, Canoga Park, California 91304, USA.

SLEC, Units 8-10, Norwich Road Ind. Est., Watton, Norfolk IP25 6DR, England.

Southeast Model Products, 14325 60th Street North, Clearwater, Florida 33520, USA.

Sterner Engineering, 661 Moorestown Drive, Bath, Pennsylvania 18014, USA.

Steve Korney, 14835 Halcourt Avenue, Norwalk, California 90650, USA.

Supersonics P.O. Box 691810, Tulsa, Oklahoma 74169, USA.

Thorjet, 4 Main Street, Glaston, Oakham, Leicestershire, LE15 9PB, England.

Turbofan, 5 St. Johns Road, Clevedon, Avon, BS21 7TG, England.

VTH, GmbH, Postfach 1128, 7570 Baden-Baden, West Germany.

Webra Modellmotoren Gmbh and Co., KG, Eichengasse 572, A-2551, Enzesfeld, Austria.

Yellow Aircraft and Hobby Supplies Ltd., Suite 201, 3040 Palstan Road, Mississauga, Ontario L4Y 2Z6, Canada.

Zack-o Plastics, P.O. Box 1082, Folsom, California 95926, USA.

APPENDIX 2
DUCTED FAN REFERENCES

MAG.	LOC.	YR.	MON.	PAGE	No Ps	TYPE	CONTENT	AUTHOR
FM					1	COL.	THORPE PLANS/KRESS	KULCZYK
AMMO		62	3	24	3	REV.	FAN EXPERIMENTS	NORMAN. PE
RCME		72	12	785	7	CONS	EPEE	NORMAN
URCM		76	6	56	4	REV.	FAN DESIGN 1	SCOZZAFAVA
URCM		76	8	44	4	REV.	FAN DESIGN 2	SCOZZAFAVA
URCM		77	3	64	4	REV.	FAN DESIGN 3	TICHENOR
URCM		77	10	81	6	REV.	FAN DESIGN 1	KRESS
URCM		77	11	66	5	REV.	FAN DESIGN 2	KRESS
URCM		78	4	66	6	REV.	FAN DESIGN 3	KRESS
URCM		78	5	58	5	REV.	FAN DESIGN 4	KRESS
SRCM		78	8	44	6	KIT	JHH MIRAGE	VAN OWEN
URCM	★ ★	78	9	39	3	KIT	VIOLETT A4 SKYHAWK	
RCME		79	9	851	2	COMP	OLD WARDEN 79	RUSSELL
RCMB		79	11		3	REV.	FAN DESIGN 1	KRESS
RCMB		79	12	34	3	REV.	FAN DESIGN 2	KRESS
RCME	SP	80	0	44	5	REV.	SCALE SPECIAL	WHITEHEAD
RCMB		80	1	40	3	REV.	FAN DESIGN 3	KRESS
UMAN		80	3	25	4	KIT	VOILETT A4 SKYHAWK	FARRELL
UMAN		80	3	30	5	REV.	RK20B FAN	SARPOLUS
FM		80	3	23	7	CONS	TOMMYCAT	FARKAS
FLUG		80	4	334	4	CONS	ALPHA JET	VOSS
FLUG		80	4	346	2	REV.	FAN DESIGN	VOSS
RM		80	5	60	4	REV.	FANS ETC. 1	NORMAN
URCM		80	5	40	4	KIT	HOB SABRE	TICHENOR
RM		80	6	44	6	CONS	MIG-15	NORMAN
RCME		80	6	576	3	REV.	GENERAL 1	RUSSELL
URCM		80	6	36	4	REV.	RK-20 FAN	ZDANKEWICZ
SRCM		80	7	44	7	KIT	BYRON F16	GAULT
RM		80	7	35	3	REV.	FANS ETC. 2	NORMAN
RCME		80	7	700	2	REV.	GENERAL 2	RUSSELL
SRCM	★ ★	80	8	51	6	KIT	A4 SKYHAWK	FRANKEL

UMAN		80	9	24	4	KIT	BYRON MIG	NEWBOLD
SRCM		80	10	42	8	KIT	BYRON MIG	CROWE
RCME		80	11	1118	3	CONS	DELTA 1000 RK20B	DENNETT
UMAN		80	11	24	4	KIT	JHH COUGAR	PERKINS
URCM		80	12	16	7	CONS	STAR COBRA	BRIDGES
MOAV		81	1	58	2	REV.	KRESS TANDEM .09	SARPOLUS
URCM		81	2	46	2	REV.	RK-20 FAN	URAVITCH
RCMB		81	3	32	2	KIT	BYRON MIG	JOLLY
SRCM		81	4	50	13	COMP	US MASTERS	
RM		81	4	29	1	REV.	FANS USA	HOLL
UMAN		81	4		1	REV.	ITALIAN F86	CHINN
SRCM		81	8	36	7	COMP	FUNFLI	
RM		81	9	55	3	COMP	ABINGDON 81	
RCME		81	10	926	2	COMP	ABINGDON 81	BODDINGTON
URCM		81	11	14	2	KIT	BYRON MIG	
RM		81	12	48	4	CONS	PANTHER	NORMAN
URCM		81	12	68	5	COMP	ABINGDON 81	WHITEHEAD
RCME		81	12	1163	3	REV.	FANS ETC.	BODDINGTON
URCM		82	1	38	4	COMP	US MASTERS	TIANO
URCM		82	1	76	3	CONS	CITATION	TICHENOR
SRCM		82	2	33	15	COMP	US MASTERS	
MODL		82	2	88	2	REV	BAUER FAN	VOSS
SRCM		82	2	22	5	COMP	ABINGDON 81	AYERS
SRCM		82	4	42	10	KITS	TWO SABRES	VENTOLA
URCM		82	6	53	2	KIT	JHH COUGAR	
UMAN	★ ★	82	6			CONS	TOMCAT 1	GUPTON
SKYP		82	7	41	1	CONS	NORMANS JAVELIN	GRAY
UMAN	★ ★	82	7			CONS	TOMCAT 2	GUPTON
UMAN		82	7	68	5	CONS	HOB SABRE	SCHROEDER
SRCM		82	8	50	13	COMP	UNCONTEST F-18	
UMAN	★ ★	82	8			CONS	TOMCAT 3	GUPTON
SRCM		82	8	66	2	CONS	BLACKBIRD	VAN OWEN
RM		82	9	20	2	COMP	ABINGDON 82	
SKYP		82	9	8	3	REV.	GENERAL 1	GRAY
URCM		82	9	48	3	KIT	JHH T. SHARK	HEADLEY
URCM		82	9	45	3	COMP	WORLD SCALE	TICHENOR
FM		82	10	40	4	REV.	½ A DUCTED FANS	SARPOLUS
IMOD		82	10	577	6	CONS	ITALIAN F100	CASSAMALI
RCME		82	10	883	2	COMP	ABINGDON 82	BODDINGTON
SKYP		82	12	44	7	REV.	GENERAL 2	GRAY
RCME		83	1	26	4	CONS	HAWK	GRAY
RCMB		83	2	22	8	KIT	BYRON A4 SKYHAWK	
SRCM		83	2	34	13	COMP	US MASTERS	
SKYP		83	2	29	3	REV.	GENERAL 3	GRAY
UMAN		83	3	13	3	COL.	FANS KITS	URAVITCH
UMAN		83	4	50	3	COMP	US TANGERINE	
SKYP		83	4	31	3	REV.	GENERAL 4	GRAY
UMAN		83	6	28	2	REV.	VOILET SABRE	URAVITCH
UMAN		83	7	52	4	COMP	MIG 8TH SS	PARSONS
FLUG		83	7	606	4	REV.	FANS A10	WEIKING

SRCM	83	8	42	9	KIT	COOK PHANTOM 1	COOK
UMAN	83	8	51	2	COL.	FANS	URAVITCH
RM	83	9	18	2	COMP	ABINGDON 83	
FLUG	83	9	778	3	CONS	A-10 THUNDERBOLT	WEIKING
RCOM	83	9	40	6	REV.	FANS COMPARISONS	RATAJCZAK
SRCM	83	10	27	9	KIT	COOK PHANTOM 2	COOK
UMAN	83	10	66	6	KIT	BYRON A-4	URAVITCH
UMAN	83	10	70	4	COMP	D. FANS USA	URAVITCH
RM	83	10	40	3	KIT	FANJETS HAWK	SPREADBURY
MODL	83	11	710	3	COMP	A-10 AT ARTLAND	
FLUG	83	11	334	2	COMP	A-10 AT ARTLAND	HARTWIG
UMAN	83	12	36	4	COMP	BYRON FAN-FLY	
URCM	83	12	67	5	COMP	US NATS	
UMAN	83	12	86	5	COMP	US NATS	
UMAN	83	12	102	1	COL.	HYPERFAN	CHINN
URCM	83	12	24	12	CONS	VIGILANTE	FRANKEL
MOFL	83	12	582	3	COMP	D. FANS GERMANY	OHLGART
SRCM	84	2	49	10	COMP	US MASTERS	
MOAV	84	2	90	3	REV.	FULL-SIZE FAN DEV.	PALUMBO
RCME	84	2	128	4	CONS	VIGGEN	GHISLERI
UMAN	84	3	30	2	COL.		URAVITCH
SRCM	84	4	34	10	KIT	COOK PHANTOM	HANSEN
UMAN	84	5	67	6	CONS	TOMCAT 1	KOLISCO
UMAN	84	6	59	7	CONS	TOMCAT 2	KOLISCO
IMOD	84	6	19	5	CONS	ITALIAN F84	CASSAMALI
RM	84	7	18	3	REV.	GENERAL F16	THORPE
RCMW	84	8	44	2	REV.	GENERAL	NYE
UMAN	84	8	36	5	CONS	TOMCAT 3	KOLISCO
SRCM	84	8	22	5	KIT	JHH CORSAIR	PERKINS
UMAN	84	8	26	1	COMP	ABINGDON 83	URAVITCH
RCMW	84	8	40	4	COMP	ABINGDON 83	SPREADBURY
URCM	84	9	88	3	COMP	KFIR IN SCALE COMP.	CLAYMAN
UMAN	84	9	42	2	COL.	RK-740 ETC.	URAVITCH
RM	84	9	42	3	COMP	ABINGDON 84	BODDINGTON
URCM	84	10	32	15	CONS	CHINOOK	GILLESPIE
FM	84	11	28	4	COMP	BYRON FAN-FLY '84	FANELLI
FLUG	84	11	966	2	COMP	ABINGDON/SWEDEN	WEIKING
UMAN	84	11	66	4	COMP	BYRON FAN-FLY '84	URAVITCH
FLUG	84	12	1038	3	CONS	F106 DELTA BOSS 602	WEIKING
MODL ★★	85	1	9	3	COMP	HILLERSE FAN-FLY 84	VOSS
UMAN	85	1	28	10	CONS	F-84F THUNDERSTREAK	MUSCIANO
UMAN	85	1	14	2	COL.	FOREIGN NEWS	URAVITCH
SRCM	85	2	30	9	KIT	WLD ENG TIGERSHARK	SPINUZZI
UMAN	85	2	35	2	COL.	FOREIGN NEWS	URAVITCH
RCMB	85	2	11	4	COMP	S.W. FAN-FLY USA	VON JETSKI
RM	85	3	26	4	REV.	DUCTED FANS PT.1	THORPES
UMAN	85	3	26	2	COL.	S.W. FAN-FLY USA	URAVITCH
UMAN	85	4	54	4	KIT	BYRON SABRE	TIANO
SRCM	85	4	30	11	CONS	A-10 WARTHOG	MILLER
FM	85	4	31	3	COMP	SW (USA) FAN-FLY	FRANKEL

RM	85	4	54	5	REV.	DUCTED FANS PT.2	THORPES
SRCM	85	4	38	10	COMP	US MASTERS '85	WEHMEULLER
URCM	85	5	32	12	CONS	F-100 SUPER SABRE	JOHNSON
RM	85	5	52	3	REV.	DUCTED FANS PT.3	THORPES
UMAN	85	5	30	2	COL.	COOKE DYNAMAX FAN	URAVITCH
RM	85	6	50	4	REV.	DUCTED FANS PT.4	THORPES
UMAN	85	6	47	2	COL.	WRAM SHOW	URAVITCH
RM	85	7	22	5	CONS	F-86 SABRE	THORPES
UMAN	85	7	38	2	COL.	FAN BALANCER	URAVITCH
RM	85	8	49	1	CONS	F-86 SABRE SUPP.	THORPES
RCMW	85	9	50	3	KIT	TURBOFAN F86 SABRE	WELLER
UMAN	85	9	14	2	COL.	NEW FANS	URAVITCH
RM	85	9	46	2	COMP	ABINGDON '85	BODDINGTON
SRCM	85	10	52	7	COMP	BYRON JET RALLY '85	GOYER
FM	85	10	31	5	COMP	BYRON JET RALLY '85	FANELLI
RCMB	85	10	23	3	COMP	BYRON JET RALLY '85	FRANKEL
UMAN	85	10	66	3	COMP	BYRON JET RALLY '85	URAVITCH
URCM	85	10	126	4	COMP	BYRON JET RALLY '85	TICHENOR
RCMB	85	12	15	4	KIT	BYRON (NEW) MIG-15	CROWE
SRCM	85	12	16	4	REV.	BYRON INTERVIEW	DEVON
RM	85	12	43	3	COMP	SWEDISH SCALE NATS.	JAMES
SRCM	85	12	68	2	KIT	KNIGHTS/AIR U2 PT.1	ALSTAR
SRCM	85	12	12	4	CONS	M-27 PRESSURE JET	FRANKS
UMAN	85	12	44	2	COL.	NEW MODELS	URAVITCH
URCM	86		134	4	COL.	ARCHIVE. S.W. FAN-FLY 85	JOHNSON
RMOD ★ ★	86	1	34	2	KIT	MIRAGE	RABE
SRCM	86	2	58	3	REV.	JET-AGE MODELS	CAMILLE
FM	86	2	30	4	COMP	S.W. FAN-FLY USA	FANELLI
FM	86	3	71	1	COL.	FAN-FACTS HISTORY	KULCZYK
UMAN	86	3	64	4	COMP	S.W. FAN-FLY USA	URAVITCH
FM	86	4	72	1	COL.	FAN TEST-BENCH	KULCZYK
UMAN	86	4	46	3	COL.	NEW MODELS/KITS	URAVITCH
UMAN	86	5	60	4	KIT	KNTS/AIR TIGERSHARK	HUYNH
FM	86	5	72	1	COL.	FAN TESTS	JONES
UMAN	86	5	38	4	KIT	VIOLETT SPORTSHARK	TIANO
SRCM	86	5	10	3	KIT	JMI (GERMAN) F-16	WENDT
SRCM	86	5	34	5	COMP	JETS AT FUNFLYS	CELESTE
FM	86	5	78	1	COL.	FAN NEWS	KULCZYK
FLUG	86	5	14	4	REV.	IMPELLER NEWS NO.2	WEIKING
SRCM	86	5	26	7	KIT	COOKE F-4 PHANTOM	FIORENZE
UMAN	86	5	24	2	COL.	TURBOFAN SABRE	URAVITCH
FM	86	6	78	1	COL.	NEW FANS	KULCZYK
UMAN	86	6	69	5	KIT	J.H.H. F-86 SABRE	PERKINS
UMAN	86	6	60	2	COL.	WRAM SHOW	URAVITCH
RM	86	7	48	2	REV.	FANS IN USA	JAMES
FM	86	7	70	1	COL.	FAN NEWS	JONES
FM	86	7	70	1	COL.	FAN FACTS	JONES
RCMB	86	7	21	4	REV.	DUCTED FAN OVERVIEW	FRANKEL
SRCM	86	7	32	17	CONS	SAAB VIGGEN	THACKER
UMAN	86	7	52	2	COL.	NEW FANS	URAVITCH

Mag.		Yr	Mo	Pg	No	Type	Title	Author
SRCM		86	8		99	BOOK	SCALE JETS 86	GOYER
MODL	★★	86	8	506	3	CONS	F-86 R.81 BYROJET	THOMA
RCME		86	8	592	3	CONS	THORJET FAN	PETRIE
FM		86	8	73	1	COL.	RECENT GOSSIP	FANELLI
FM		86	8	71	1	COL.	BD-5J ETC.	KULCZYK
RCME		86	8	564	1	COL.	TURBOFAN MIG-15	RUSSELL
UMAN		86	8	56	2	COL.	BEDE/JHH SABRES	URAVITCH
FM		86	9	31	1	COMP	WRAM/TOLEDO JETS	FANELLI
FM		86	9	70	2	COMP	CANADIAN FAN-FLY	FANELLI
FM		86	9	70	2	COL.	CANADIAN JET RALLY	FANELLI
MODL	★★	86	10	681	4	COMP	KARBACH FAN-FLY	VOSS
FM		86	10	70	1	COL.	FAN BALANCING	JONES
RCME		86	10	730	2	COMP	ABINGDON 86	PETRIE
RCMB		86	10	12	4	COMP	CANADIAN JET RALLY	FRANKEL
SRCM		86	10	52	12	CONS	AVRO ARROW	PARKINSON
FM		86	10	38	4	CONS	BYRON F-16 TO XL	MUNNINGHOF
SRCM		86	11	34	10	COMP	BYRON JET RALLY 86	GOYER
RCME	SP	86	11	52	2	COMP	ABINGDON 86	JAMES
SRCM		86	11	11	9	KIT	BYRON F-15 EAGLE	CELESTE
FM		86	11	34	5	COMP	BYRON JET RALLY 86	FANELLI
RCMB		86	11	28	5	COMP	BYRON FAN-FLY 86	FRANKEL
RM		86	11	52	2	KIT	TURBOFAN F86 SOARER	STEADMAN
MAN		86	11	28	4	COMP	CANADIAN JET RALLY	URAVITCH
FM		86	12	70	1	COL.	FAN LINKAGES	JONES
SRCM		86	12	70	2	CONS	TWIN BYROJET HORNET	LOPES
RM		86	12	20	7	CONS	THUNDERBOLT A-10	WATERS
URCM		87		126	4	REV.	BYROJET/ROSSI TUNE	THACKER
FM		87	1	71	1	COL.	FAN CONTROL	JONES
SRCM		87	1	10	5	REV.	FANS IN ENGLAND	SWEENEY
UMAN		87	1	32	2	COL.	GOSSIP	URAVITCH
FM		87	2	34	5	COMP	S.W. FAN-FLY '86	FANELLI
RCMB		87	2	45	5	COMP	S.W. FAN-FLY	FRANKEL
FM		87	2	73	1	COL.	VIOJETT	KULCZYK
FM		87	3		1	COL.	OTHER DESIGNERS	KULCZYK
UMAN		87	4	94	2	KIT	VIOLETT AGGRESSOR	TIANO
FM		87	4	34	3	CONS	BOSS 602 FAN	WALKER
UMAN		87	4	40	3	KIT	BYRON KFIR	THACKER
FM		87	4	71	1	COL.	FAN RELIABILITY	FIORENZE
SRCM		87	5	31	13	COMP	'87 TANGERINE	GOYER
FM		87	5	70	1	COL.	VECTORED THRUSTS	KULCZYK
RCME		87	5	350	1	COL.	ELECTRIC FANS	PEACOCK
UMAN		87	5	30	3	COL.	PHANTOMS	URAVITCH
FM		87	6	70	1	COL.	THRUST PENDULUM	KRESS
RCMB		87	6	24	2	COMP	SW FANFLY PHOTOS	FRANKEL
SRCM		87	6	36	7	REV.	CLOUD DANCERS	VELOSKY
UMAN		87	6	64	4	COMP	'86 SW FANFLY	URAVITCH
RCME		87	6	476	1	COL.	A-COOPERS HARRIER	RUSSELL
RCMB		87	7	19	5	KIT	VIOLETT SPORTSHARK	FRANKEL
RCMW		87	7	67	1	COMP	FANS AT SWINDERBY	PEARSON
UMAN		87	7	52	2	COL.	WRAM '87 SHOW	URAVITCH

RCMB		87	7	19	5	KIT	VIOLETT SPORTSHARK	FRANKEL
FM		87	7	70	1	COL.	TURBAX I IMPROVED	KULCZYK
RCMW		87	8	9	2	COMP	ABINGDON '87	EDITOR
UMAN		87	8	60	5	KIT	BYRON F-15 EAGLE	FRANKEL
UMAN		87	8	56	2	COL.	VIOLETT/STERNER	URAVITCH
MODL		87	8	498	4	REV.	GLEICHAUF FAN	VOSS
FM		87	8	70	1	COL.	VECTORED THRUST	HUNT
RCME		87	9	700	2	COMP	ABINGDON '87	BODDINGTON
MODL		87	9	570	3	COMP	KARBACH '87	VOSS
MOFL		87	9	432	3	COMP	KARBACH '87	OHLGART
RM		87	9	63	3	COMP	ABINGDON '87	JAMES/SPDY
FM		87	9	44	3	COMP	TOLEDO '87	FANELLI
FM		87	9	24	7	CONS	PHANTOM PT.1	BAUGHER
FM		87	9	70	1	COL.	DIESEL ENGINE DFAN	FRANKEL
SRCM		87	10	26	3	COMP	ENGLISH JETS	SWEENEY
FM		87	10	70	1	COL.	OLD STYLE JETS	KULCZYK
UMAN		87	10	26	6	COMP	CANADIAN FANFLY	URAVITCH
FM		87	10	46	4	CONS	PHANTOM PT.2	BAUGHER
SRCM		87	11	50	4	CONS	PHANTOM	THACKER
SRCM		87	11	18	4	COMP	ABINGDON '87	SWEENEY
UMAN		87	11	52	2	COL.	VARIOUS	URAVITCH
FM		87	11	70	2	COL.	CG. COMPUTER PROG.	STERNER
RM		87	12	63	3	REV.	FAN RELIABILITY I	JAMES
FM		87	12	73	1	COL.	SEWELLS BD-5J	KULCZYK
RCMB	★ ★	87	12	20		COMP	CANADIAN FLY-IN '87	
RM		88	1	16	3	REV.	FAN RELIABILITY 2	JAMES
SRCM		88	1	53	5	KIT	BYRON F-15	RUFF
FM		88	1	30	3	COMP	CANADIAN FLY-IN '87	FANELLI
FM		88	1	33	2	COMP	SW FANFLY, COPELAND	FANELLI
FM		88	1	35	3	COMP	ABINGDON '87	WALKER
UMAN		88	1	32	2	COL.	MILLER PHANTOM	URAVITCH
RCMB		88	1	23	6	COMP	SW FANFLY 87	FRANKEL
RM		88	2	16	3	REV.	TRANSATLANTIC FANS	JAMES
URCM		88	2	268	4	COMP	ABINGDON '87	SPREADBURY
UMAN		88	2	44	2	COL.	FORCE-AIR FAN COMP	URAVITCH
UMAN		88	2	52	1	COL.	JHH F-86 AEROBATICS	LEE
FM		88	2	70	1	COL.	MODEL TURBINES	JAMES
RCOM		88	2	99	7	COMP	EUROPEAN FLY-INS	AVONDS
SRCM		88	2	16	5	KIT	BLUE HORNET	PARKINSON
SRCM		88	3	29	5	KIT	JHH PHANTOM	CAMILLE
SRCM		88	3	34	8	CONS	DRONE TURBINES	GOYER
RCMW		88	3	54	1	COL.	KUESTER TURBOJET	MILLER
UMAN		88	3	44	6	COL.	SW FANFLY '87	URAVITCH
RCMB		88	3	18	5	COMP	WESTONZOYLAND '87	SWEENEY
RM		88	4	48	2	COMP	WESTONZOYLAND '87	JAMES
SRCM		88	4	50	6	CONS	VARIOUS TIGERSHARKS	PRICE
FM		88	4	70	1	COL.	FIBREGLASS REPAIRS	THOMPSON
UMAN		88	5	60	2	COL.	GOSSIP	URAVITCH
RM		88	6	15	1	COMP	CANADIAN FLY-IN '87	
SRCM		88	6	16	6	REV.	HURRICANE FANS	PRICE

SRCM	88	6	46	15	CONS	CUSTOM F8 CRUSADER	MILLER
UMAN	88	6	32	7	KIT	BYRON BD-5J	SCHROEDER
UMAN	88	6	66	4	COMP	TANGERINE TOP GUN	ZOBER
FM	88	6	70	1	COL.	WRAM SHOW '88	FANELLI
FM	88	7	68	2	COL.	WRAM SHOW '87	FANELLI
RCMW	88	7	37	3	COMP	SWINDERBY '88	THOMPSON
SRCM	88	7	12	3	REV.	INTERVIEW G. MILLER	EATON
SRCM	88	7	34	11	REV.	TOLEDO '88	GOYER
RM	88	8	44	2	CONS	HARRIER PT.1	KOSKELA
SRCM	88	8	10	2	COL.	NEW D/F COLUMN	MILLER
RCMW	88	8	49	3	COMP	ABINGDON '88	PEARSON
SRCM	88	8	20	2	CONS	THORPES OF ENGLAND	GOYER
SRCM	88	8	28	6	CONS	F-104 STARFIGHTER	THORPE
RM	88	9	16	2	COMP	ABINGDON '88	TRESTRAIL
RM	88	9	18	2	CONS	HARRIER PT.2	KOSKELA
UMAN	88	9	66	6	COMP	CANADIAN FLY-IN '88	URAVITCH
UMAN	88	9	32	3	COL.	NEW KITS	URAVITCH
FM	88	9	70	1	COL.	D FAN FLY-INS	KULCZYK
RCME	88	10	796	3	COMP	ABINGDON '88	SPREADBURY
MODL	88	11	783	2	COMP	NEUSTADT '88 FANFLY	VOSS
FM	88	11	74	2	COL.	THRUST TESTS PT.1	SWEENEY
SRCM	88	11	32	7	CONS	JET ENGINE	GOYER
SRCM	88	11	50	6	CONS	MIG-21 FISHBED	FARRELL
SRCM	88	11	23	2	COL.	DF CONST.N TIPS	MILLER
RCMB	88	12	16	5	COMP	ABINGDON '88	SWEENEY
FM	88	12	70	2	COL.	THRUST TESTS PT.2	SWEENEY
UMAN	88	12	44	3	COL.	NEW PRODUCTS	URAVITCH
SRCM	88	12	40	9	COMP	DF BYRON EXPO '88	GOYER
UMAN	89	1	36	2	COMP	F-18 MASTERS WINNER	FIORENZE
RCMW	89	2	50	3	COMP	GRTR SW FANFLY '88	RICHMOND
SRCM	89	2	10	2	CONS	BOOZ JET TURBINE	PRICE
SRCM	89	2	20	21	COMP	'88 SCALE MASTERS	GOYER
RM	89	3	46	5	CONS	SMALL DUCTED FANS	TRESTRAIL
URCM	89	3	190	4	CONS	LEARJET 35A	FRANKEL
URCM	89	3	54	2	COL.	FUTURE FANFLYS	SCHAFER
FM	89	3	36	3	COMP	SWINDERBY '88	SWEENEY
FM	89	3	39	3	COMP	BELLEVILLE '88	FANELLI
FM	89	3	42	3	COMP	SW FANFLY '88	FANELLI

BOOKS:

1955	'AEROMODELLER ANNUAL' Single Chapter, P.E. NORMAN.
1969	'FLYING SCALE MODELS' Chapter 11, MOULTON.
1974	'AEROMODELLER ANNUAL' Single Chapter, M. NORMAN.
1981	'BUILDING AND FLYING DUCTED FAN AIRCRAFT' Kalmbach USA, SARPOLUS.
1985	'IMPELLER PRAXIS FUR FLUGMODELLE' VTH W. Germany, WEIKiNG.
1986	'SCALE JETS '86' Challenge Publications USA, GOYER (Editor).
1987	'R/C DUCTED FANS' Motorbooks International USA, FANELLI.

KEY TO ABBREVIATIONS.

AMMO	American Modeller (USA)
FLUG	Flug Modelltechnik (GERMANY)
IMOD	Modellistica (ITALY)
MOAV	Model Aviation (USA)
MODL	Modell (GERMANY)
MOFL	Modelflug (GERMANY)
RCMB	Radio Control Model Builder (USA) now called Model Builder
RCME	Radio Control Models and Electronics (GB) (SP = Scale Special)
RCMW	Radio Control Model World (GB)
RM	Radiomodeller (GB)
SKYP	Skyplane (GB)
SRCM	Scale Radio Control Modeller (USA)
UMAN	Model Airplane News (USA)
URCM	Radio Control Modeller (USA)
RCOM	Radio Commande Magazine (FRANCE)
FM	Flying Models (USA)
RMOD	R.C. Modelle (GERMANY)
REV.	Review article
KIT	Kit review
CONS	Construction article
COMP	Competition, Fly-in, or Trade-show
COL	Regular column
LOC ★ ★	Not available to Turbofan
MON.	Month
YR.	Year
No.Ps	Number of pages

INDEX

Abingdon Fly-in 159
Aerodynamic balancing 112
Aerodynamic centre 85
Aerofoil 102
Aerojet fan 44, 46, 67, 156
Ailerons 105
Air filter 69
Air Flair Manufacturing 151
All flying tail (AFT) 111
Anderson, Lee 58
Area ruling 29, 30, 58, 102
ART F kits 161
ASP Plans Service 157
Astley-Cooper 162
Auxiliary systems 80, 117-127
Avonds, Philip 92, 102, 147
Axial drive impeller 53
Axiflo 52, 55
Balancing fans 130, 131
Bauer 18, 46, 47, 51, 61, 69, 69, 149, 157
Baughers, Eric 157
Bellmouth inlet 29
Belt starter 134
Berkeley Models 12, 20
Bertella 157
Billinton, Mike 31, 70
Blade tip clearance 39
Blades 32
Blow-in doors 89
Bob Diveley Model Aircraft 151
Bob Parkinson Flying Models 147, 157
Bombs 123, 156
Boss fan 18, 19, 31, 32, 37, 46, 47, 67, 68, 155
Brakes
  dive or air 105
  wheel 122
Brodbeck, John 63, 64
Byrojet 20, 32, 48, 51, 52, 60, 67, 69, 70, 73, 81, 124, 134, 148, 151, 153, 155
Byron Originals 19, 48, 92, 117, 118, 125, 152, 159
Canard 113

Canopy, opening 124, 125
Cantelli, Aldo 52
Carbon fibre 114
Catapult (bungee) launch 139
Century Jet Models 152
Centre of gravity 81, 84, 99, 106, 111, 112, 113, 142
Chart-Micromold 53
Cheat inlet 81, 87-92, 145
Chinn 31
Climb (rate and angle) 108, 109
Control surface (wing) 105
Conway, Barry 98, 137, 138
Cook, Tom 49, 155, 160
Cooke, Ian 60
Cornish-Trestrail, Alec 42, 126, 150, 161
Crashes 128, 129
Custom R/C aircraft 153
Davies Diesel Developments 51
Dennett, Graham 157
Design of fan 35, 36
Deutscher Modellflieger-Verband (DMVF) - 161
Diesel 51
Dihedral 104, 110
Dolly 95, 141, 156
Doors (for landing gear) 98, 99
Drag 102, 107, 110
Drogue parachute 124
Droop nose 127
Drop tank 123
Drum rotor 69
Duct collapse 34
Ducts 99-102
Dutch roll 110
Dynamax 28, 49, 66, 67, 69, 149, 151, 152, 154, 155, 157
Dynamic (velocity) pressure 89, 138
Dynamic thrust 27, 37, 38, 91, 107, 110
Efficiency 28, 29, 30
Effinger, Bill 12
Electric power 160
Elevator 111

Empennage 110-114
Engine cover cap 100
Epifiano, Larry 44
Exhaust port timing 63, 72
Fan characteristics 35
Fanjets 20
Feedthrough bellcrank 132
Fence (wing) 105
Fibreglass 114
Fin 110
Finishing techniques 114
Fiorenze, Bob 124, 148, 155
Flaps 105, 142
Flight log 128
Flutter 104, 112
Flying ducted fans 139-146
Flying Modeller (magazine) 157
Fly-ins 159
Foam 116
Foam inlet 46, 48
Force Air 49, 50
Frankel, Mark 125, 157
Friction (on ground) 144
Fuel-proofing 116
Fuel supply 117, 131, 135
Fuselage lift 84
Gallena, Norbert 157
Gas Turbine 8, 9, 10, 162
Ghisleri, Alberto 157
Glass fibre 114
Gleichauf 51, 52, 69, 148, 149
Glockner, S 157
Glow plug 77, 78, 136
Godberson, Byron 69
Golds, Chris 21, 94, 115, 124, 126, 127
Grey, Paul 157
Gupton, Norman 157
Hand launch 139, 160
Harrier (VTOL) 161
Harris, G W W 13
Hatches 92
Hobby Barn 153
Holman, Bob 157
Horizontal stabilizer 111-113
Horsepower 31, 33
House of Balsa 155
H R Modelltechnik 46, 149
Hurricane fan 32, 51
Hyatt Tech 153
Hyperfan 52
Imp 12
Impeller rpm 36
In-flight mixture control 69, 119
Inlet duct 100
Inlets 81, 87-92
Inspection and testing 129-132

Irvine 73
Jackman, Gerry 10, 162
Jet Age 53, 106, 153
Jet Hangar Hobbies 17, 20, 57, 92, 154
Jet Model Products 49, 154, 155
Jet Pilots Organisation 161
Jetex 13
John Carpenter Models 150
Johnson, Art 157
Johnson, Einar 97, 98, 113
K & B 63, 64
K B V 64
Kits 147-157
Knights of the Air 155
Korney, Steve 51
Koskela, Mike 161
Kress, Bob 17, 18, 25, 29, 39, 40, 44, 55,
    60, 87, 137, 158
Kress Jets 64
Krick Modellbau 150
Kyosho 150
Landing gear 95-99, 141
Landing procedure 143
Leading edge extension 85, 105
Lift, coefficient 102, 103, 145
Lindsey, Kevin 72
Lyco, K B 46
Manufacture 43, 44
Marles, Dave 72
Materials 43, 44, 114
M D M 155
Mean chord 85
Micromold 20, 32, 33, 37, 53, 54, 55, 59,
    150, 161
Midwest Products 155
Miller, George 153, 157
Mini-pipe 74
Model Airplan News 157
Modifications to fans 60
Multi-engines 123
Musciano, Walter 157
Needle valve 119, 120
Newton, Sir Isaac 17, 25, 29
Nipple (pressure) 75
Nitromethane 63, 72, 78, 136
Noise 74, 160
Norman, M 11, 15, 17, 20, 37, 54, 157, 158
Norman, P E 11, 13, 15, 16, 54, 158
Oleo legs 96
O P S engines 66, 75
Optional systems 122
O S engines 66
Outlet diameter of fan 27, 38
Overheating (of engine) 78
Paul's Flying Stuff 155
Picco 68

Pilot error 129, 145
Planform (wing) 103
Plans 157
Pressure rise across fan 33
Pressurised fuel tank 74
Pumps (fuel) 74, 117
Purcell Jnr, Thomas H 12
Radio Control Modeller Magazine 157
Radio control system 120-122, 130
Ram effect 88-90
Ramair fan 161
Rear exhaust 63
Rear induction 63
Reliability 128-132
Remote needle valve 119
Retracting undercarriage 96, 104
Reynolds Number 40
R K fans 17, 18, 37, 44, 46, 53, 54, 55, 59,
    60, 66, 87, 155, 156
Robart 132
Rockets 124
Rolf Gleichauf 51
Romair 97
Rossi 68, 69, 70, 73
RPM measurement 136
Rudder 111
Saldivar, Ralph 60
Sarpolus, Dick 155
Scale R/C Modeller (magazine) 157
Scale speed 109
Scozzafarva, James 17, 158
Scozzi 17, 18, 57, 63, 87
Servo fixing method 121
Servo load 112, 122
Short, Sqd Ldr 13
Silencing 74, 160
Simons, Martin 103, 107
S L E C 32, 130
Smith, Phil 11, 12
Smith, Reg 123
Smoke system 125
Solidity ratio 35, 36
Southeast Model Products 44, 156, 157
Spoilers 105
Stability 110
Stall of fan blades 38
Stall (of wing) 103, 113, 145
Starter extension 134
Starting, engine 133
Static thrust 27
Stator efficiency 36
Stipa-Caproni 11
Struck 11
Sullivan Pylon brand fuel tank 119
Supercharging 24
Supersonics 156

Sweeney, Ron 56, 57, 92, 101
Swept wing 103, 104
Swing-wing 106
Swirl 36
Tailpipe outlet diameter 38
Tailplane 111-113
Take-off techniques 139, 140
Thacker, Bob 32, 60, 157
Theory of fans 24-42
Thorjet 20, 55, 56, 66, 68, 109, 157
Thorpes, Peter and Paul 21, 55, 89, 141,
    156, 157
Throttle linkage 132
Thrust line 83
Thrust measurement 136-139
Thrust-reverser 126, 127
Thrust-to-weight ratio 79, 108, 109, 138,
    140, 162
Tse, Dr Jack 21, 22, 145
Tuned pipe 63, 71-77, 117, 131, 136, 160
Tuning, engines 136
Turbax 17, 18, 25, 55, 57, 66, 67, 68, 69, 80,
    133, 154, 155, 156
Turbofan 20, 33, 51, 55, 64, 73, 114, 123,
    150
Tyson, Dave 161
Undercarriage 95-99, 104, 141
Vacuum forming 116
Vector fan 161
Vectored thrust 109, 162
Velocity of air through fan 34, 35
Veron 11, 12, 13, 20
Vertical stabilizer 110
Vibration 121, 136
Violett 17, 20, 22, 23, 29, 30, 38, 64, 92,
    96, 102, 134, 145, 151, 160
Viojett 23, 28, 29, 30, 33, 34, 38, 58, 64, 67,
    80, 118, 119, 121, 134, 139, 151
Voss, Heinrich 157
V T H (W Germany) 157
V T O 109, 161
Washout 102
Waters, Trevor 156, 157
Webra 70, 71
Whittle, Sir Frank 8, 24, 159
Wing design 102-110
Wing loading 80, 85, 145
Wisniewski, Bill 72
Wolfe, Larry 20, 58, 92, 124, 154
Woods, Harry 125
World Engineering 155
Yellow Aircraft and Hobby Supplier 148
Zero contraction tailpipe 28
Zia models 153
Ziroli, Nick 156, 157

Subscribe now...

here's 4 good reasons why!

Within each issue these four informative magazines provide the expertise, advice and inspiration you need to keep abreast of developments in the exciting field of model aviation.

With regular new designs to build, practical features that take the mysteries out of construction, reports and detailed descriptions of the techniques and ideas of the pioneering aircraft modellers all over the world – they represent four of the very best reasons for taking out a subscription.

You need never miss a single issue or a single minute of aeromodelling pleasure again!

	U.K.	Europe	Sterling Overseas	US Dollar Overseas
Aeromodeller *Published monthly*	£23.40	£29.80	£31.90	$58
Radio Modeller *Published monthly*	£19.20	£25.90	£28.10	$51
RCM&E *Published monthly*	£20.40	£28.50	£31.50	$57
Radio Control Scale Aircraft *Published bi-monthly*	£15.00	£19.20	£20.60	$38

Your remittance with delivery details should be sent to

Argus Subscription Services
Queensway House, 2 Queensway,
Redhill, Surrey RH1 1QS